D0361345

THE ZERO FOOTPRINT BABY

WITHDRAWN
FROM
COLLECTION

THE ZERO FOOTPRINT BABY

HOW TO SAVE THE PLANET
WHILE RAISING A HEALTHY BABY

KEYA CHATTERJEE

PUBLISHING

BROOKLYN, NEW YORK

Copyright © 2013 by Keya Chatterjee
All rights reserved.

Printed in the United Sates of America.
First Paperback Edition
10 9 8 7 6 5 4 3 2 1

No part of this book may be used or reproduced in any manner
without written permission of the publisher.

Please direct inquiries to:
Ig Publishing, Inc
392 Clinton Avenue
Brooklyn, New York 11238
www.igpub.com

Library of Congress Cataloging-in-Publication Data

Chatterjee, Keya.
  The zero footprint baby : how to save the planet while raising a
healthy baby / Keya Chatterjee.
      pages cm
  Includes bibliographical references.
  ISBN 978-1-935439-65-3
  1. Child rearing. 2. Sustainable living. 3. Carbon dioxide-
-Environmental aspects. I. Title.
  HQ769.C423 2013
  649'.1--dc23
                              2013008012

To my guys, with all my love. You make life a joy and an adventure.

CONTENTS

Introduction   9

1. Building Your Nest   19

2. Prenatal Care and the Birth of Your Child   43

3. All That Baby Gear   61

4. Are Cloth Diapers A "Clothian" Bargain?   73

5. Feeding the Beast (Baby)   91

6. The Child Care Dilemma   109

7. Family Size: How Much Is Too Much?   121

8. The Adoption Option   133

9. Bringing Others On Board   145

10. Nap Time Activism   157

Epilogue: Our Zero Footprint Baby   169

Appendix   174

Acknowledgements   177

Notes   178

INTRODUCTION

"Some scientific conclusions or theories have been so thoroughly examined and tested, and supported by so many independent observations and results, that their likelihood of subsequently being found to be wrong is vanishingly small. Such conclusions and theories are then regarded as settled facts. This is the case for the conclusions that the Earth system is warming and that much of this warming is very likely due to human activities."
—The National Academy of Sciences, May 19, 2010

Before we became parents, my husband Andrew and I had built a relatively sustainable life. We ate food grown on a local farm, and only bought used clothing. We sold our car and used public transportation to get around town. (Andrew also ran five miles to work each day, while I biked to my job.) We commissioned a home energy audit, insulated our house, and recycled our most energy intensive appliances, which meant we lived without a clothes dryer, and—to most people's astonishment—a refrigerator. In the winter, we kept produce and dairy products in a cooler on our back patio, while in the summer, we were careful to sequence our meals so that we ate all the quick-to-spoil leafy greens early in the week, followed by other vegetables that lasted longer, and lastly, dried foods like lentils and rice or pasta. (We discovered that eggs did not need to be refrigerated at all, regardless of the season.) We never wasted food, since everything we had was always sitting on our counter in plain sight, reminding us to eat it before it went bad. We dug a compost pit in our backyard for our vegetable peels and coffee grounds. We also installed solar panels in our backyard that covered our home energy use. We were even contemplating going off the grid altogether. In short, we tried not to use more resources on the planet than we could replace in our lifetimes. Some people count calories; we counted kilowatts. Living sustainably had become a game for us, and we were getting quite good at it.

And then we decided to have a baby.

Almost immediately, people started asking how we were going to manage raising a child with the confines of our lifestyle. "You MUST be getting a refrigerator and a car now?" they would ask, or, "I guess that means you're giving up on reducing your carbon footprint?" And most devastatingly, from our hardcore environmentalist friends, "Isn't having a baby inconsistent with addressing climate change?"

Finding myself without answers to these kinds of questions, I went about researching how to raise a baby without increasing our family's carbon footprint. I started this quest with the hope that a baby, at least in its first year, could come without any increased pollution. There is a saying that two people can live on less than one, and I was about to find out if those economies of scale could be applied to three.

I immediately discovered that there was no central place to find what I was looking for. I found some stuff on the internet, while other information came from my immediate family members, or from the experiences of friends I knew in the environmental vanguard who were raising kids. Some of the answers I found by digging into my heritage in India, where families generally practice more sustainable lifestyles than they do in the United States, such as not using diapers. I amused my mothers' friends to no end by prodding them to remember every detail about infant pooping practices that they had left behind in India when they immigrated to the United States a lifetime ago. Other solutions turned out to be more high tech, like the superefficient refrigerator that we had custom-made for us in Silicon Valley, an appliance so efficient that even the energy of having it trucked across the country was negligible relative to the high-energy consumption of the next-best option. Overall, however, I found it difficult to find information about the carbon footprint of the most basic decisions that most expectant parents face, like how to diaper, what you "need" to buy, and what to feed your baby.

As a result of this lack of information, I decided to write this book. In the following pages, you will find a compilation of the diverse information I collected so that we could make it through the first year of our baby's life without raising our family's carbon footprint by even one pound. Each chapter is an amalgam of the research that I did in order to reach a particular parenting decision, combined with the stories of my family and other families we know. I've pulled all this information together in one place so that you and yours don't have to comb through scientific journal articles about the life cycle assessment of different products, or spend hours on the internet trying to decipher foreign cloth diaper terms, all the while wondering if cloth diapers are even any better than disposables in terms of pollution.

Why Consider A Zero Carbon Footprint Baby?

Like most new parents, sometimes when I watch my son Siddharth as he sleeps, my eyes well up with tears. And it's not just because I'm exhausted and he's *finally* asleep. It's because I so want the best for him. I want him to grow up on a clean, safe and healthy planet. I imagine a future for him that offers just as many opportunities as I was provided as a child. I want him to be able to see Glacier National Park while there is still a bit of glacier left there, and dive in coral reefs before they are bleached. It concerns me that when Siddharth is an adult, a ninety degree day will barely be considered noteworthy in our hometown of Washington DC.[1] It's scary to think about the future impacts of global warming on the planet he will inhabit—more children heading to the emergency room with asthma attacks during heat waves and poor air quality days, 100-year floods hitting more than once a lifetime, rising sea levels encroaching on our coasts, acidifying oceans killing our coral reefs, sea ice melting at stunning rates. It makes me sad to think of the large number of deadly extreme weather events my son will either experience or watch unfold on TV. Just between 2006 and 2012, for example, four out of five Americans were affected by weather-related disasters.[2] I can't help but imagine how hard it will be for Siddharth to grow up in a world where he is exposed to so much climate-induced devastation.

While the enormity of the climate crisis should be enough to frighten any person, as parents, we have made a decision that many believe is inherently part of the problem: we have decided to have children. The assumption has always been that more people on the planet leads to more climate change. That may be true, especially if our children continue to engage in the same type of activities that produce greenhouse gas pollution. On the other hand, it is possible to use the birth of our children as a catalyst to change the way we live and the actions we demand of our government. Through the way we raise our children, we can set an example for how society as a whole can be more sustainable, in the process making people less afraid of the environmental policies and new attitudes that we need in order to secure a safe future for our children.

I should say right up front that our individual acts as parents alone will not save the planet. However, when families act, it creates the enabling conditions for good environmental policy, as well as helping existing policies reach their full potential. One of the main barriers to sound legislation to tackle climate change is an overall societal fear that we cannot thrive economically while reducing our pollution. By modeling parenting behavior that creates less pollution, we have the power to prove that it is possible to reduce our pollution dramatically and have our families thrive at the same time. We can show others that there are viable alternatives to our addiction to fossil fuels, for example. We can dare people to imagine a society where we raise our babies in a way that helps the planet. We can speak with our communities and our elected representatives on these issues more comfortably once we have made changes in our own lives. Using the suggestions in this book, your family can reduce, or even eliminate, the additional carbon pollution associated with your baby's first year. By having a low—or zero—carbon footprint baby, parents can reduce their family's greenhouse gas pollution, and in so doing, leave their child the best gift a parent can give—a safer planet.

Why Focus On Carbon Pollution?

To date, the parenting literature has been largely silent about climate change, even though it is the most important issue in our children's future, more important than their diets, education, or interpersonal relationships. It is more important than ensuring that we use BPA-free plastics, non-toxic cleaners, and eat organic food, even though those are all good things. The reason it is so important is because none of these other things will matter if our children do not inherit a stable climate that can provide food and water security. Thus, the benefits are enormous if parents decide to take actions to ensure that we leave our children and our children's children a habitable planet. The consequences are equally enormous if we do not act. Tackling climate change is not a fanciful hope that I have; it is a core part of my job as a parent.

While any kind of pollution is bad, this book is focused on carbon footprints, which are a measure of greenhouse gas pollution. Greenhouse gas pollution is not your parents' pollution. The main difference is that the toxic pollutants that the environmental movement of the 1970's was responding to could actually be cleaned up. These pollutants made a mess, yes, killing people and destroying ecosystems. But with enough money and effort, you could usually restore things to pretty much the way they had been before. In 1969, for example, the Cuyohoga River in Ohio caught fire due to floating chemical-soaked debris, but thanks to the Clean Water Act and other legislation, today fish are coming back to a river that was once filled with toxic metals like cadmium, chromium and lead. Unfortunately, both the Clean Air Act and the Clean Water Act are currently under attack, with proposals being introduced regularly to scale back these landmark laws and prevent them from being used to solve today's biggest environmental threat, greenhouse gas pollutants.

The planet's atmosphere is a very thin layer that is uniquely capable of supporting life. "Greenhouse gas" pollutants are named for the Greenhouse Effect, in which gases trap heat in the atmosphere, causing average global temperatures to rise. At natural concentrations, greenhouse gases are a good thing— they keep our planet warm. However, we are now putting greenhouse gases into the atmosphere at a much faster rate than the plants on the planet can remove them, causing a build-up that is disrupting the climatic conditions under which human beings evolved. Imagine the atmosphere as a bathtub. We are putting greenhouse gas emissions into the tub faster than the bathtub drain can remove them. This process is not sustainable, as eventually the bathtub will overflow, water will get into the floorboards and the ceiling below will collapse. While we don't know exactly how big the bathtub is, we do know that it is quite full, and that we are nearing the capacity of our atmosphere to safely absorb all the excess pollution. Imagine another analogy, of a cyclist riding a bike down a foggy steep mountainside and suddenly realizing there is a cliff ahead. He knows the cliff is there, but the fog prevents him from seeing exactly where it is. The most logical thing to do is to hit the brakes. This is the situation we are in as a society. And yet, we are not hitting the brakes. Not only are we not passing legislation to tackle climate change, we are continuing to subsidize fossil fuel use, and provide oil companies with tax shelters and other special treatment.

While we fiddle, the climate continues to change, responding to the increase in greenhouse gas pollutants in our atmosphere in both predictable and unpredictable ways. Even the best-case scenarios for the future include more frequent or severe extreme weather events and food insecurity for the most vulnerable. The relationship between climate change and extreme weather is a bit like the relationship between speeding on the highway and car accidents. If you are going 180 mph, you are more likely to get into an accident. Accidents are also more severe at such a high rate of speed. As we are changing the climate, we are increasing the frequency and severity of extreme weather (i.e. accidents).

Just like with a car accident, assigning blame is not simple when it comes to extreme weather. If the driver was texting and speeding, was it the texting or the speeding that caused the accident? If the driver was also drunk, do we then say the speeding didn't matter, and it was the alcohol that caused the accident? Unless we outfit all automobiles with a "black box" that we analyze after each accident, we can never be certain exactly what caused the accident. In the same way, it takes a lot of analysis to determine if climate change played a role in any given extreme weather event, but we know that as a whole, these events would not be as bad if we were not disrupting our climate. In addition to the difficulty of assigning blame for specific events, it is also difficult for scientists to show people the problems associated with greenhouse gas pollution, because once the pollutants are in the atmosphere, they are largely odorless and colorless.

Unfortunately, these pollutants are disrupting our climate, and they persist for much longer periods of time than traditional pollutants. CO_2, the most common greenhouse gas, stays in the atmosphere for over a hundred years. On top of all this, in the United States—the country that has contributed the most to global greenhouse gases—there is a vocal minority that rejects climate science, which hinders the government from passing effective policies to price or regulate pollution. Despite evidence to the contrary, the fossil fuel industry wants to make sure that no one believes climate change affects extreme weather and public health, in the same way the tobacco industry fought hard to try to muddy the linkage between smoking and lung cancer.[3] For now, the problem is being ignored by policy makers, leaving individuals to figure out how to avoid the status quo and force action on this issue. Fortunately, catalytic events like Superstorm Sandy, the extreme drought in the middle of the US, and larger wildfires are starting to change the complacency among the public and policy makers alike. Society is beginning to realize that we must curb our carbon pollution.

How Is A Carbon Footprint Calculated?

The term "carbon footprint" was coined in 1999 to refer to the amount of greenhouse gas pollution caused directly or indirectly by a person. The term is a bit confusing because it uses the word "carbon," but this kind of pollution is not measured in units of carbon, but rather in units of *carbon dioxide equivalents (CO2e)* per year, a unit that includes both the impact of carbon dioxide and the impact of other greenhouse gases like methane and nitrous oxide. (In this book, I use the term "carbon" as shorthand for CO2e in places for ease of writing. Carbon is actually lighter than carbon dioxide.) Since greenhouse gas pollution can be both released into the atmosphere and removed from the atmosphere (by planting a tree, for example), a person's carbon footprint can be calculated as the amount of pollution they are responsible for creating, minus the amount that, through their actions, they remove. Actually calculating a carbon footprint is a bit complex, but there are many online calculators that do the job. And while the concept is relatively simple, experts can argue around the edges about what should and should not be included. It's also important to note that many of the numbers used for calculating carbon footprints are approximations. They are, however, the right order of magnitude, and are good enough to get a general sense of the impact we are having on the planet.

For the purposes of this book, I assume a person's carbon footprint to include the sum of carbon pollution from:

A) Home energy use

B) Transportation

C) Materials purchased

D) Food

E) Workplace energy

F) Personal share of federal, state, and local emissions

I then subtract the carbon pollution that people remove from the atmosphere or prevent from being released into the atmosphere from:

G) Planting trees

H) Recycling materials that would otherwise be releasing carbon in the trash

I) Generating excess renewable energy to be used by others

J) Reducing the amount of energy that a person might cause other people to use (such as your parents, if you are a newborn) in housing, transport, or food

(A+B+C+D+E+F) minus (G+H+I+J) equals your carbon footprint. A "zero carbon footprint" refers to the situation in which the result of this equation is zero. (You directly control all of these numbers except, perhaps item F, which refers to the pollution created by our government.)

A "zero carbon footprint baby" is a baby whose first year of life results in relatively little additional household and community pollution from A through F, and whose parents welcome the baby into the world by maximizing G through J. Put this way, a "zero carbon footprint baby" sounds like an arithmetic problem, but it is really much more than that. By working towards reducing our carbon footprint, I felt like I was doing my job as a parent to protect Siddharth's future. I also felt more honest when I spoke to others about the need to act and the need to pass policies to tackle climate change. I felt confident calling my member of congress and asserting that we owed it to our kids to tackle climate change. My personal efforts, and my story, strengthened my resolve to protect my son's future and stand up to people attempting to threaten it.

As I see it, there are three steps to achieving climate change: (1) taking action yourself; (2) encouraging action in your community; and (3) joining the national movement of parents who are demanding policies to tackle climate change. This book will provide you with the information that you need to do all three of these things, with a focus on the decisions that you make in the first year of your baby's life. This is a particularly critical time because many of the decisions that parents make during pregnancy and the first year of their child's lives lock in their carbon emissions for years to come. It is also a particularly exhausting time for new parents, so it is ideal if you can start this journey even before your baby is born, go slowly, and give yourself a break sometimes. Do what you can. Don't worry about what you can't do. Even if you only do one or two things in this entire book, you are still helping to ensure your child a safe and healthy future.

1. BUILDING YOUR NEST

"Life is always a rich and steady time when you are waiting for something to happen or to hatch."—E.B. White, *Charlotte's Web*

A general rule of thumb in many parts of the world today is that the more kids you have, the more likely you are to lead a high-carbon lifestyle. Having children often results in families living farther from work, social centers and public transportation—thus becoming more reliant on a car. Having children also often results in families buying a larger home that uses more heating and air conditioning, or having relatives who travel more frequently by automobile or plane to visit you and your children. The carbon footprint of living in our houses, and getting to and from those houses, is a major contributor to our nation's enormous portion of global greenhouse gas pollution. In the United States, buildings and transportation together account for more than sixty percent of greenhouse gas emissions.[1] With per capita emissions in this country at around twenty tons of CO_2e per person, if you assume that the footprint of individuals has a similar breakdown to that of the economy as a whole, approximately twelve of those tons are coming from buildings and transportation.[2]

Understandably, none of this matters much to the hormone-crazed, power-nesting pregnant woman (I once heard a story of a woman who was vacuuming her home's unfinished attic space in the ninth month of pregnancy), or the safety-crazed expectant father (think child-proofed cabinets awaiting mother and new baby). At worst, these instincts can lead to comically ill-timed decisions to replace roofs, gut kitchens, and even move whole houses during a pregnancy. But it's not just nesting instincts that are at fault for these types of decisions. There is also a societal push to "trade up" houses in anticipation of starting a family, and a belief that the baby will require a great deal more space than the twenty or so inches of its body. Apart from wanting more physical space, new parents understandably also want to be in the best school district, have a yard for their children to play in, and a safe neighborhood to come home to. Unfortunately, the fallout of child-related moves tends to be more energy-intensive commutes to work and more floor space in houses to heat and cool, all of which lead to higher energy use and an increased carbon footprint.

Nothing shapes a baby's carbon footprint more than the actions of their parents. In the early months of your child's life, you as parents are already making decisions that will affect your baby's carbon footprint for years to come. For example, deciding to stay in our hometown, and in the same home, after Siddharth was born so that we would not need a car was one of the most important decisions we made about his carbon footprint. While most of the "green tips" for new parents focus on the most eco-friendly toys for our children to play with and the best organic foods for them to eat, the size, efficiency and location of a baby's home will have a much larger effect on their carbon footprint than anything they eat, play with, or wear in the first year of their lives. For that reason, the decision of whether to remodel, move, or stay in your current house is extremely important to your baby's carbon footprint. Think of it this way: choosing the right home (if you are moving), or the right type of renovations (if you are staying), is a gift to your child that will keep on giving.

The same nesting instincts that prompt expectant parents to move or remodel their homes can be channeled into choices that reduce our carbon footprints and show the world that living without pollution is normal and nothing to fear. If we see the Earth as the ultimate nest for our babies, we can then make decisions that will prepare the planet for a sustainable future. For example, we have the technology and resources available to dramatically decrease the carbon footprint of our houses during this nesting period, in the process creating homes that produce less greenhouse gas pollution than those that we lived in before having children. Unfortunately, the reality is that even as we stumble out of the bathroom with a positive pregnancy test in hand, our happiness is already tinged with panic about our living situation when the baby comes in nine months:

"We live in a studio apartment. Where are we going to put this baby and his or her stuff?"

"Once we have this baby we will never have the time or money to renovate this disgusting kitchen and put in an open floor plan with granite countertops."

However you react to these fears, building the right nest for your family has the potential to dramatically decrease your carbon footprint. But to have a "zero footprint baby," it is essential that your home at the very least *not increase* your carbon footprint in the first year of your child's life. To compensate for small increases in your carbon footprint elsewhere, ideally the carbon footprint of your home should decrease even as you increase the number of people living in it.

Our Nesting Story

As a Peace Corps volunteer in Morocco in the late 1990's I rented living space from a family of eight in a small village and sometimes slept in their single room house along with the rest of the family.

The quarters were tight, but it was more than enough room to lay back, and a cozy place to be on cold nights.

More than a decade later, my husband Andrew and I found ourselves living in a bigger space than we had ever imagined. The crazed housing market of the early 2000s made it nearly impossible to buy a condominium unit because most places were selling the minute they hit the market. After being too slow to the draw a few times, we finally bought a 1,200 square foot townhouse in a lesser-known part of Washington DC that was near public transportation. We had a lot more room than we needed for just the two of us, so when I got pregnant, I already knew that we did not require any additional space. I felt the nesting instinct strongly, however, and worked to prepare our home for our baby during most of my waking hours. I was definitely not the only one feeling the nesting urge. One day as I was cleaning a closet, my husband was tinkering around in our bathroom. I knew he had wanted to fix a drip from the toilet, so I assumed he was replacing a seal in the toilet tank. Much to my astonishment, when I walked into the bathroom, I found it empty, and I don't mean that my husband had gone. He was there, but NOTHING else was, as the bathroom no longer had a toilet or a sink—it was now an empty shell! Apparently, Andrew had started fixing the toilet, but when he realized it was beyond repair, he took it out, which tore up the floor. When he went to rip up the floor, part of it was stuck under the sink, so he took out the sink. And so on. I wasn't able to hear his explanation clearly because all I was thinking about was how I was just a few weeks away from having our baby and we had no bathroom!

Luckily, we were able to take advantage of my husband's destruction to do an extreme green makeover on our bathroom. We quickly installed the most efficient toilet and sink, which meant that we starting flushing 70 percent less water right at the time that we starting hosting more guests in our home who were coming to see our new baby. Before I knew it, we had saved enough water to make up for the carbon associated with discarding the old bathroom items. This led me to start thinking about what else we could green in our home as part of our nesting phase.

Remodeling Your Home

In the bleary-eyed, early-morning haze of new parenthood, it is very hard, if not impossible, to think about the carbon footprint of your every action and its impact on the planet you will be leaving to your tiny little baby. That's why the nesting phase is so important to your success in having a zero footprint baby. Done correctly, this phase can put many of your carbon emissions reductions on auto-pilot. For example, as a new parent, you won't need to think about how to make your lights more efficient if you have already installed LEDs. A 2010 study showed that people overestimate the benefits of their conservation actions dramatically, and *underestimate* the benefits of buying more efficient appliances and gadgets.[3] Turning out the lights when you leave the room and turning off the water while you brush your teeth are not as effective as buying LED light bulbs and low-flow faucets. As a parent, you have a lot going on, and could really run yourself ragged making sure the lights are off and the bath is not running for too long. You can have a greater impact by investing in one-time actions like upgrading your water heater and replacing light bulbs. Although we already had solar panels and insulated double honeycomb blinds in our home, we found that we still had a lot of changes to make during our nesting period. We used the time before our son was born to get LED light bulbs, purchase the most efficient ceiling fans, dishwasher, and washing machine on the market, and install a low flow shower head and sink faucets. Whether adding insulation, upgrading windows, installing solar panels, eliminating entertainment and communication equipment, or replacing an inefficient refrigerator, remodeling with the environment in mind reduces your carbon footprints for a long time to come.

If you have already done your home remodel and it involved importing granite from Asia, buying wall-sized TVs, and adding rooms, it's still not too late to turn things around and pursue a low-carbon path. Fortunately, we now have more information than we have ever had about ways to do "zero-footprint nesting." Energy Star standards exist for appliances and houses, the Green Building Council certifies buildings through its LEED certification program, and websites like toptenusa.org provide consumers with information about the most efficient appliances on the market. We also know how to make net-zero energy houses that are passively heated and cooled. The basics are simple: insulate your house, use less heating and cooling, produce renewable energy on-site, have few appliances, and when appliances are necessary, have the most efficient ones. In short, focus on the actions that can make a big impact on your carbon pollution, that will automate energy savings in the future, and which are visible to a world which needs to see that reducing one's pollution is not a scary or impossible proposition. Nesting can not only be carbon-neutral, it can be carbon-negative, in the sense that you can dramatically reduce your household carbon footprint from what it was before pregnancy.

If you don't have money to spend on renovations, remember that some behaviors can be just as important—especially behaviors that eliminate the need for high energy-use appliances or reduce the amount space or the degree to which you are heating and cooling your home. Whether or not you are able to buy a more efficient laundry machine, you can always line dry your clothes inside or outside. We don't own a dryer, and while it takes more time, we save money and pollution by line drying our clothes. The great thing about line drying is that it keeps you in tune with the weather. We pay close attention to whether it looks like it will rain, and what time of day will be warmest. Line drying our clothes also allows us to quickly see which things need mending. In short, line drying produces more benefits for us than just reducing our pollution; it is a part of our identity and our lifestyle. That's true for almost every change we have made to reduce our carbon pollution.

Even if you can't install geothermal heating and cooling in your home, you can still change the setting on your thermostat. In our family, a cooler home meant more winter mornings sharing hot cups of tea and coffee under a blanket, and more time with the baby snuggled close to us in a carrier. In the summer, it meant more time at the community swimming pool and the neighborhood fountains. It's true that everyone has limitations, but it's also true that everyone can do more. Focus on the things that you can do within your budget and housing circumstances. And, most importantly, don't stop at just one thing. There is a phenomenon known as "single action bias," which indicates that most people will only take one action in support of the environment and then feel that they have checked off the box on being an "environmentalist." People will change their light bulbs, for example, and then decide they have done what is necessary, even if their home is still an energy hog. This is why I suggest that rather than have the goal of doing one thing, your intent should be the broader aim of getting your carbon footprint as low as possible.

Don't Sweat The Small Stuff (but it's not all small stuff)

There are three areas you should focus on to reduce your home's carbon footprint:

1. Heating, Ventilation and Air Conditioning (HVAC). Upgrading your air handler or air conditioner to the most efficient model has an outsized impact on the environment.

2. Building Envelope. When your are heating your home in the winter, you don't want all that warm air to seep out of the house. You can keep it in by improving insulation and window treatments. You can also plant a tree outside

of your house, which will provide shade in the summer but lose its leaves in the winter to let the sun shine in to help warm your home.

3. Refrigeration. The refrigerator is probably the only appliance in your home that does not have an off switch. Replacing your old refrigerator with the most energy efficient model is a significant action. Also, consider reducing the size of your refrigerator and freezer. In recent decades, refrigerator size has gone up while family size has gone down (and this has correlated with waist size increases, as well).

Our Home Energy Audit

I had wanted to do a home energy audit for a long time, and when I received a phone call from the city that our turn had for a government-sponsored audit, I scheduled one as soon as possible, and even took the day off of work. When the auditor from Honeywell arrived, he asked for a tour of the house. He pointed out that since we lived in a co-op, and didn't own the building we lived in outright, some of the most important changes, such as insulating the roof and painting it a light color, were not undrr our control. Since there was nothing I could do about the roof, I asked him to give me some tips about how to save energy in the rest of the home. He walked around the pointed out all of the places where cold air from outside was coming in—the kitchen fan, around the windows, around the outlets, at the bottom of our sliding glass door. He also inspected the basement and told us it could use more insulation, and he suggested that we look into a programmable thermostat.

A couple of weeks later, we got the notes from the inspection in the mail. While there was nothing in there that we didn't already suspect was a problem, it was nice to have a complete list of issues that needed to be addressed. It was also helpful because the memo gave me fodder to ask our co-op for changes. For example, I had previously asked for permission to have our kitchen fan insulated and dry-walled over, but my request had been denied. However, once I had evidence that it was wasting energy (and I showed that I had purchased two additional smoke detectors), I was allowed to cover up the old leaky kitchen fan. After the fan, I tackled the windows. I already had double honeycomb blinds, but I added winter shrink wrap covering on the windows and doors for the winter, and caulked up all the cracks that the auditor had pointed out to us.

A Zero Footprint Pregnancy Calendar For Home Renovations

First Trimester

The first trimester is a time for evaluation and planning:

> Get a home energy audit professionally done and start monitoring your energy bills. Many utilities or local governments will help you with the cost of an energy audit and assist you in finding professionals in your area. Look for home energy auditors who are certified as "BPI Building Analysts." In addition, search for incentives and contractors working with the "Home Performance with Energy Star" program.

Initiate the changes that will take the longest amount of time, such as:

> Getting your building to give units control over heating and cooling.

> Installation of new items in your home or within your condo or co-op. Start early because this will take some time. The list of items that require planning includes: insulation, new windows, solar panels, green roofs, wind turbines, and smart meters.

Start measuring your home's electricity with a smart meter or other device that measures details of home energy use. Contact your utility company and find out if you can have a smart meter installed that will record your electricity use throughout the day. If a smart meter is not available, you can still monitor the daily fluctuation in your energy use using something like a TED (The Electricity Detector), a device that attaches to your circuit breaker and comes with a small digital display that shows your energy use. If you have solar panels or a wind turbine, a TED or smart meter will also measure how much electricity you generate.

Form an eco-team. Identify friends and neighbors who might also be interested in lowering their carbon footprint and start to meet with them on a regular basis. A good guide for your group's activities is a book called *The Low Carbon Diet*.

Second Trimester

Since most of the first trimester nausea has usually passed, the second trimester is usually the time when pregnant women have the most energy to focus on renovations. Take this time to implement any major changes.

Install more efficient appliances that will reduce the power you spend controlling the temperature of your home, and on warming or cooling your food, laundry, and dishes. There are enormous energy savings to be found in replacing inefficient air handlers, refrigerators, washing machines (you will soon be doing more laundry), etc. At a minimum, choose Energy Star appliances. Ideally, buy the most efficient appliances available commercially by checking www.toptenusa.org or looking at the detailed tables of data provided by the Energy Star program.

Complete energy and insulation installations (e.g. solar panels and foam insulation).

Caulk up all spaces between the walls and floors, windows and doors, and even around outlets. You can always open windows and use fans on days when you are not heating or cooling the house if things get stuffy. If you live in an older home with a furnace or boiler, double check to make sure those devices have a "make up air valve" in place. (If you have a professional home energy audit done, they should check for this.)

Start composting. If you have a backyard, dig a small ditch to use for food scraps (wear gloves or get someone other than a pregnant woman to do this). You can also use a store-bought compost barrel—many attractive varieties are available. Don't have a yard? Is there a community garden where you can dig a ditch for coffee grounds and tea at least? A balcony for a worm compost bin? There are also indoor composters, but they require a bit more maintenance and should be turned on every day to prevent moisture build up and odor.

Third Trimester

As you are getting bigger, make sure your carbon footprint is on track to get smaller. For some women, the nesting instinct will really kick in around this time, so you may end up doing more than the small projects outlined here.

Switch to green energy by contacting a company that can provide 100 percent wind energy or other renewable options. Visit the "Green Power Network" operated by the Department of Energy, which can help you find a retailer in your area that will sell you green energy.

Install clothes drying lines inside and outside your home and wash all your (used/borrowed) baby clothes.

Eliminate or unplug entertainment devices that use energy even when they are not in use, like video game consoles. New "smart plug" power strips are designed so that when you turn off your TV, you can also automatically turn off all the attached appliances. Over the past few decades, appliances have become more efficient per square foot in the US, but the problem is that energy use has still gone up thanks to increases in home and TV size, computers, and the energy draw of TV-related devices like DVRs and gaming consoles.[4] Keep in mind that televisions and computer games are not recommended for small children, and they waste energy.

Install an efficient showerhead, faucet aerator, or a smart faucet to reduce water wastage on sinks.

Consider installing grey water catching devices such as a "toilet sink" that lets you wash your hands with clean water before it fills the toilet tank, so you can flush your toilet with grey water.

Toilet Sink

When I originally searched for a toilet sink, the only ones I found were used stainless steel models that, for some reason, had been previously used in prisons. There were a few of them on Ebay, and they looked like municipal water fountains with a toilet seat attached. While I liked the idea, my mother refused to use a toilet that had come from a prison, plus the device looked cumbersome to install. Eventually I found a brand called the "SinkPositive" which takes only a few minutes to install and remove, and even works for renters. The SinkPositive replaces your regular toilet lid with a sink and retails at around $100. It can either be installed in addition to the regular sink, or if you don't have room for a sink in a second bathroom, it can provide a sink in a small space. I have one friend who installed a toilet in her basement with only a SinkPositive sink because of her space constraints.

Here's how it works: Under normal conditions, your toilet tank fills up with clean potable water that the city you live in has spent energy making drinkable. Since you don't need drinking-water quality to flush the toilet, a SinkPositive prevents the clean water from entering straight into the toilet and instead directs it into the sink spout so that you can use it to wash your hands. The "grey water" that is dirty from your hand washing then fills up the toilet tank, and the next time you flush, you are using grey water to flush instead of clean water. As soon as you flush the toilet, clean water will shoot out of the sink for you to wash your hands. The timing is convenient, since you'd be turning on the sink to wash your hands right after flushing anyway. As the website for SinkPositive says," Fresh water for your hands, grey water for the bowl."

The Zero Carbon Remodel

Don't be satisfied with using things like salvaged wood and recycled cork in your remodel. While these make a remodeling effort less resource intensive, they do not lower the carbon footprint of your home going forward. Focus all of your efforts instead on actions that will reduce your carbon footprint dramatically—heating and cooling systems, refrigeration, and making sure that your home is not drafty by using the most effective insulation and caulk. Explain to your contractors why you are lowering your carbon footprint, and when possible, make your actions visible to the outside world. Whenever my husband and I make a change in our home, we ask ourselves if it will reduce our carbon footprint. If the answer is yes, we make the change. (Buying more efficient appliances was the most common change we made before our son was born.) If the answer is no, and the change does not reduce our carbon footprint, we spend a little more time thinking about whether we really need to do it, and whether we can pair the action with another change that would reduce our carbon footprint.

With any of the changes below, the energy associated with the renovation will be much less than the energy savings you will generate in the future:

Install the most efficient insulation on the market

Replace your current refrigerator with an energy efficient model

Replace your heating and cooling systems with the most efficient options

Start producing renewable energy by installing solar panels, wind turbines, or geothermal heating.

Moving

While many families choose to remodel the houses they live in, others decide they need to move in order to accommodate their new baby. If you move into an efficient and/or smaller house, that home will become an asset in your low-carbon efforts. However, if you move into an inefficient and/or larger home, it will be difficult to overcome that liability as long as you own that house. The reason is that most energy use by families is tied to the size of their home. Since 1950, the average house in the United States has grown from 983 square feet (SF) to 2,434 SF, according to the National Association of Home Builders, while the average family size has gone down over that same time period.[5] Families in other countries manage to live in smaller spaces than we did even in the 1950's, and not surprisingly, they generally have lower carbon footprints.

Apart from the reduced carbon footprint, another advantage of smaller homes is that you won't need things like a baby monitor, since you will be able to hear the baby just fine no matter where you are in the house. A bigger house not only necessitates a baby monitor, but it also uses more resources to build and requires more energy to run. Heating and cooling large homes is especially hard on your carbon footprint, and larger homes also have more light bulbs, appliances, and a larger likelihood of containing a second refrigerator.[6] Despite increased energy efficiency of the appliances that heat, cool, and light our homes, nationally, we are producing more pollution on heating, cooling, and lighting simply because our homes are getting larger.[7]

Nonetheless, not everyone will be comfortable room-sharing or co-sleeping with their baby in a studio apartment. If new parents feel like they need to set aside a room for their baby, it is still possible for them to reduce their carbon footprint by focusing on moving to a home that has both energy efficiency and the right location.

Heidi's House Size Story

My husband and I met Heidi in a book club on sustainability that we joined when we were first thinking about whether or not to have a child. At the time, Heidi had a four year-old son, and her story was fascinating to us because it was so different from the stories of many of our friends who had children and had moved to larger houses. Heidi's story started the same as theirs, but didn't end the same.

After scrimping and saving for years, Heidi and her husband were able to move out of the city and buy a small three-bedroom house in the suburbs when she became pregnant. The house was large enough for a separate room for the baby, as well as another bedroom in case they decided to have a second child one day. While Heidi and her husband had to buy a car since they could no longer walk to get groceries and other necessities, and couldn't afford to go out as much because they had spent so money on the house, at first the tradeoffs seemed well worth it.

Then their son was born, and Heidi found herself stuck alone in the house. Since gas prices were high, she couldn't afford to drive that much, compared to the past when she lived in the city and could walk anywhere she wanted to. Being trapped in a house with a new baby became difficult for Heidi. After a year of living in the suburbs in what they thought was their dream house, Heidi and her husband cut their losses, putting their house on the market and moving to a one-bedroom apartment in the city.

In doing so, their lives were environmentally transformed. Living in the city meant they now had plenty of access to parks and other outdoor spaces. Reducing the size of their home also cut their housing expense to a third of what they had been. Instead of needing several rooms, they were able to put their bed in the "living room" while the baby slept in the bedroom. In addition, the building Heidi and her husband moved to had a room that could be rented for entertaining, so they didn't have to host guests in their small apartment (and out-of-town guests could stay anywhere in the city and still easily visit the new baby.) For Heidi, less space meant a lower carbon footprint—and a happier family!

Location, Location, Location
City Mouse or Country Mouse?

On average, per capita emissions are lower in urban centers than in rural areas. However, not everyone wants to raise their kids in the city, or even in a transit-oriented town or suburb. Luckily, there are many options for rural parents who want to have zero footprint babies. To understand these options, it's worth looking a little more closely at how energy is used by both urban and rural families.

In 2009, the International Institute for Environment and Development released a report which showed that, in most cases, urban centers have fewer emissions per capita than do rural areas.[8] Advocates for rural living, who were long accustomed to thinking of cities as bastions of trash production, unnecessary infrastructure, and consumption, were astounded by these results. According to the report, it is urbanites' smaller homes and use of public transportation that combine to lower their carbon footprints relative to the country they live in. However, more recent studies in Europe have shown that when the life cycle emissions of consumed products are also included, there are rural regions that are equally or more efficient than their urban counterparts.[9]

For example, many people in urban areas consume food grown in rural areas. Once you account for the life cycle emissions of that food, including fertilizer, transport, etc., the food footprint of an urban family can be higher than that of a rural family. In fact, there is one rural island community in Denmark where residents produce more renewable energy than the community consumes.[10] As a result, that community has a much lower carbon footprint than the urban areas around it. There are other examples of this close to home. For example, the small town of Greensburg, Kansas has a lower carbon footprint than some large cities in the United States. How do they do it? They simply decided to do a green re-build after a tornado struck in 2007. Today, Greensburg has the most LEED Certified buildings per capita in the world, and the town's goal is to eventually achieve 100 percent renewable energy.[11]

One enormous advantage held by rural parents aiming to reduce their carbon footprint is their ability to acquire land for less money. Rural parents generally will have an easier time installing renewable energy because they do not have that pesky condo association to deal with that can prevent renewable energy installations, or even line drying of laundry. Space for renewable energy installations like wind turbines is available and relatively cheap in rural areas. Rural dwellers are also able to grow more of their own food and compost more easily. Finally, rural parents can manage their land so as to maximize the number of trees, thereby removing carbon pollution from the atmosphere. There are more off-grid families living in a rural setting than in urban settings simply because it is very difficult to eliminate the need for electricity if you do not have some forested land to manage for wood energy and space for wind or solar energy production.

Energy Use

If you have to move, and have settled on the perfect location for your new home, whether it be urban or rural, the next hurdle is to choose the best option for the house you intend to purchase. Unless a home is LEED certified, or is marketed as being "green," it is very hard to determine the carbon footprint of a home. While it is a niche market still, there are some real estate agencies catering to individuals interested in low carbon lifestyles, such as greenhomesforsale.com. Unfortunately, these services offer relatively little selection, and the listers self-select their homes. Still, there are some tips I can offer for finding the lowest carbon home:

1. **Find a "green" real estate agent.** A real estate agent who is LEED certified or has an ECObroker or ECO Real Estate certification can help you find a home with a low carbon footprint.

2. **Ask to see the energy bill.** Make sure you know how much energy the current homeowner uses to heat and cool the house.

3. **Bring a "Kill-A-Watt" when you tour open houses.** The Kill-A-Watt allows you to measure the energy use of any appliance. Simply plug it in to the outlet, plug the appliance to the Kill-A-Watt, and learn exactly how much the appliance is consuming at that moment. With a new baby in the house, you'll be using the washing machine a lot. Make sure it's energy efficient. Check the refrigerator, too, since it will be on twenty-four hours a day!

4. **Make sure you will have the ability to install or at least purchase renewable energy.** If the home does not already generate renewable energy, make sure that you will be able to. Check the homeowner's association/condo/co-op rules, and make sure the local policies support renewable energy.

5. **Make the home inspection a green inspection by doing a home energy audit.** In addition to the normal home inspection, hire someone to conduct a home energy audit. They will

use a device called a "blower door" to find all of the leaks in the house that need to be caulked and insulated and find any problems with the heating and cooling systems.

For Renters

When we rented our home, we couldn't do many of the things I have just talked about, either because we could not justify spending the money on a place we did not own, or because our landlord would not allow the change. Still, there are many actions that renters can take to reduce their carbon footprint that don't require large investments in a structure they don't own:

1. Rent the right place. If you are considering moving, it is the perfect time to use that move to reduce the carbon footprint of your home. Ask about utility bills and appliances before you move in, and look for places with low bills and efficient appliances. Prioritize finding a location that is transit-oriented and near your work and/or goods and services.

2. Seal your home. Get heavy curtains. In the winter, consider using shrink wrap to cover your windows. The shrink film kits run less than twenty dollars and will easily save that amount on heating bills. Make or buy a long skinny bean bag to put under your front door to prevent drafts from coming in. Consider caulking around windows and doors that are particularly drafty. While you may be reluctant to make any major investments in a rental, caulk is very cheap and can make a big difference in reducing the amount of energy you need to heat and cool your home.

3. Maintain your refrigerator and A/C unit. Clean your refrigerator coils, or ask your landlord to do it. If you have an A/C unit, make sure that it is clean as well. Turn the temperature down on your fridge and A/C so that you are only using what you need, (and not turning your vegetables into

ice.) You can also save energy on refrigeration by letting food cool before you put it in the fridge, and by keeping the fridge and freezer full of containers of water/ice so that you aren't constantly using energy to cool empty space.

4. Light bulbs, faucets, and smart power strips. Get LED light bulbs, low flow faucet heads, and smart power strips that allow you to save energy. Many of these devices take less than thirty minutes to install, and can easily be uninstalled and taken with you if you decide to move.

5. Buy green energy. If you pay your own utility bill, switch to green energy. This is possible in most states now.

6. Get involved. Find out if your local government has any incentives or educational programs designed to encourage landlords to save energy and reduce pollution, and share those resources with your landlord. If you don't pay your own utility bill, ask what percent of costs it represents, and whether there are any plans to reduce energy consumption. Make suggestions about changes to the building that could reduce pollution, and organize your neighbors to ask for these changes. If you don't live in a large building, talk with your landlord about whether they might pay for a portion of any changes that will add to the value of the building.

Transportation

Counterintuitively, living in a zero footprint passively heated house powered entirely by renewable energy is not enough to make your baby's carbon footprint zero. Instead, this would take care of only about half of your household's carbon footprint. According to a study commissioned by the Environmental Protection Agency, in the United States, an average home uses only 45 percent of its total energy to operate the house—and the remaining 55 percent for its inhabitants' transportation requirements.[12]

Taking public transportation, bicycling, or even running to your destination may not seem possible in the first few months with a baby (especially for recuperating moms!), but doing any of these will reduce your carbon footprint as well as provide great family bonding time. I did not ride my bike for almost four months after my son was born, and even after that I only rode on my own and not with him. (In the United States, most pediatricians recommend not putting a baby on a bicycle or in a running stroller until the latter half of its first year.) I did, however, take public transportation nearly everywhere. Apart from the enormous benefit to your carbon footprint, one advantage of taking public transportation with an infant is that you can feed the baby without worrying about pulling over on the side of the road or having a second passenger to help you. I was never shy about breastfeeding my son on the bus, the train, or the Metro, and I found that made getting around much easier.

Of course, public transportation is generally not an option in rural communities. As a result, rural households own more cars and drive on average 7,000 more miles per year than urbanites.[13] While rural parents can chip away at the carbon footprint of transportation by carpooling and combining trips, more dramatic reductions require replacing traditional vehicles with non-traditional ones. Bicycles may be an option for some rural dwellers who don't live far from goods and services. Electric vehicles are a super-efficient option, and are much simpler to install in rural settings than in cities, where it can be harder to find the space to install the charging system. While it is not difficult for those who live in rural areas to install a special plug point in their home, urbanites, who have to use street or garage parking, need to coordinate with city officials in order to charge an electric vehicle on a regular basis. Another option for rural homeowners with extra space for storing cars is to have a hybrid car for long distance travel and an electric vehicle for every day commuting. Since some electric vehicles have a 100 mile range, this option can be appealing to families who regularly take long distance car trips.

While replacing vehicles and addressing commutes are key elements of improving your immediate family's "location efficiency," this concept can also apply to extended family, which is particularly important for new parents who will be having many visitors during the first few months of their baby's life. Now, you may not necessarily agree that parents bear some responsibility for the carbon footprint of flights taken by relatives and friends to visit their baby, but, if you as parents hadn't decided to have children, those flights would not have occurred in the first place. As a result, as a new parent, you should do whatever you can to reduce the frequency of those flights. That may mean moving nearer to family members who are most eager to visit the baby, or else convincing family members to move closer to you. You should also consider the cost of holiday visits and vacation visits both to visit family, as well as for recreation. If you are moving for your new baby, it is worth considering whether there are ways to minimize flights, which are not all that much fun with a baby, and are the largest part of many Americans' carbon footprints.

Our Transportation Story

Although we had some tempting job offers, my husband and I decided to remain in our home, close to our extended families, when we had our son. There were several reasons for this. One, we wanted Siddharth to get to know his grandparents. Second, we did not want the carbon footprint burden of long trips that our relatives would take to visit us once we had our baby.

We already lived in a location that was easy for both sets of grandparents to visit by using public transportation—and with the lure of the baby, our parents started to use that public transportation more and more. Our parents actually got so comfortable with public transportation that they took turns coming to our house to provide childcare while my husband and I went to work. Since the baby was at home, Andrew was able to run to work and I was able to bike to work each day with my breast pump parts and bottles, and bike home with full bottles of milk.

While this was a good way to lower our daily carbon emissions, it was not enough to dramatically reduce our overall carbon footprint. To have a bigger impact, we decided to make a "one trip" pledge, meaning that, during the first year of our baby's life, we would only get on a plane for one family trip. Since s single round trip flight across the country or to Europe produces more than a ton of CO2e per passenger, this would have a big impact on our carbon footprint. Before taking the pledge, we were used to travelling four to five times a year on a plane to visit family and close friends across the country and around the world. It wasn't easy to eliminate so many trips, but we were able to do it by using our baby as an excuse. I told my colleagues at work that it was easier for me to participate in video conferences in the middle of the night than leave my baby for days at a time. We made our apologies to friends and family getting married abroad by explaining that it was just too much for us to travel with a baby. Although we were more worried about the carbon footprint of the trip than the stress of the trip, we had no regrets about avoiding long flights with our baby.

In the end, our one trip pledge worked to dramatically reduce our carbon footprint. We found places nearby to vacation and took the train whenever we could. We had to miss a few family weddings and reunions that we would have liked to attend, but we were able to use Skype and other video conferencing services to introduce our son to family and friends around the world. It wasn't an easy commitment for us, but since we didn't have many options for further reducing the footprint of our home, it was the only thing we could do that would make such a huge impact.

Zero Footprint Options
Ultimately, your home and your means of transportation are two of the areas where you can actually reduce your carbon footprint

relative to what it was before having a baby. A zero footprint baby is possible for almost everyone in the United States because we all have fat baseline pollution levels from our houses and transportation compared to other countries. The best option in housing is to either remodel your own home or move into a low-carbon footprint house. On the transportation front, the best options are to live near public transportation or use super efficient transportation such as an electric vehicle powered by renewable energy. Eliminating or dramatically reducing airplane flights will also make a big dent in your carbon footprint. Assuming you are like the average household of three and use thirty-six tons of your carbon footprint for buildings and transportation, it would be relatively easy to cut this number by 20 percent, and thereby save more than seven tons of carbon pollution from your home alone. By using the birth of your child as inspiration to make these changes to your home and your mode of transportation, you give yourself the highest likelihood of achieving a zero footprint baby.

2. Prenatal Care and the Birth of Your Child

"Birth is powerful... Let it empower you."—Anonymous

Pregnancy is a time when family and friends—as well as strangers—suddenly give themselves permission to comment on the food a mother-to-be eats, how she chooses to travel, even what she is wearing. When I was pregnant with my son, I found that people suddenly became more open about questioning my decisions when it was no longer just about my husband and I, but also about our baby. Choices about prenatal care and the birth of our baby seemed to be thought of as communal decisions that were open for discussion by all. While it is was not always easy for me to stand my ground on some of my "unusual" views—from vegetarian pregnancy to turning down an extra ultrasound—it got easier after I had done my research and felt confident in what I was talking about.

Despite this, I found that it wasn't always compelling to grandparents-to-be that there were environmental costs to extra tests and ultrasounds, as they wanted assurances about safety and health, not just the data I had been collecting on environmental impacts. Luckily, I found that that material was quite readily available too, especially from the midwifery community, which was full of information about choices that were healthy for mothers, babies and the planet. Midwives have known for a long time that fewer tests are not a danger to healthy fetuses, and that the

midwifery model of prenatal care and birth often has better out-
comes for mothers and babies alike. Ultimately, I discovered that
many of the actions I was taking to reduce my carbon footprint
during pregnancy and the birth process were also good for my
health and the health of my baby.

Midwifes, Birth Centers, and Low Carbon Births

The first thing many people did upon hearing I was pregnant was
to start giving me stuff. "Oooh, you're pregnant, hold on, let me
grab a bag of maternity clothes from my office!" I had more than
one colleague say before remembering to congratulate me on the
pregnancy. I used to joke that all those maternity clothes weren't
exactly free, because everyone who shared the clothes also required me to listen to their pregnancy and birth story! In reality,
though, I enjoyed hearing those stories, and wearing the clothes
of friends who had been pregnant before me. In addition to the
joy of receiving baby-related items than many moms had loved
and passed along, I was happy that I didn't have to buy anything
that would increase my carbon footprint.

I also found that hearing about the birth experiences of other
women with birth gave me a better understanding of what my
own options were. By talking with dozens of women in my office,
I found others who had continued their environmentally sound
practices during pregnancy. I learned about mothers who had
biked to work well into their pregnancies, and others who had
maintained a vegetarian diet. It was inspiring for me to hear their
experiences.

Many of these women had also used midwives, so I had the
opportunity to learn what midwifery was all about. I eventually
discovered that its philosophies were aligned with my minimalist ways. (My sister-in-law is a midwife, so it was a bit strange
to come to this realization from talking with others, but I had
not previously made the connection between lowering my carbon
footprint and choosing a midwife.) Once I switched to midwife-

ry care at a birth center, it became clear to me that my values were aligned with their model of care.

The birth center was affiliated with a hospital, but was a few miles away geographically (and was definitely miles away from the hospital in terms of the amount of waste it generated!) The midwives at the birth center were committed to providing me with a natural birth, without pain medication or other interventions, and were very knowledgeable about how to make that happen. Unlike the doctor I had been seeing at the start of my pregnancy, the midwives at the birth center always had an answer when I asked why a certain procedure was necessary. They too were attempting to minimize the number of tests, so we shared a common interest. They also spent more time with me than any doctor ever had, so they were able to understand my values and make suggestions that would work for me and my baby.

The birth center also targeted low income mothers, so the facility was accessible by public transportation. The public transit orientation was an important consideration for me in choosing the birth center, because most of the midwives I had spoken to were either farther away than I wanted to commute, or else their patient care model involved driving a car to my home for frequent visits. Most importantly, though, I chose the birth center because I trusted the midwives there. I trusted them to take action when it was needed, not just when it was convenient for them. I imagined a scenario where there was an emergency and my care provider was telling me that I needed to have a C-section or be rushed to the hospital. I knew that my midwives would only make these suggestions if it was absolutely necessary for my health or the health of my baby. I never quite believed that my doctor wouldn't suggest a C-section for her convenience, or due to her unfamiliarity with natural childbirth.

Of course, choosing a midwife and getting free used clothing didn't remove all of my barriers to a low carbon pregnancy. I still had to figure out how to get around, and what to eat.

My Pregnancy Biking Story

Even after I became pregnant, I continued to bike to work, just as I had been doing all along. However, at the start, it wasn't easy. During my first trimester, I was so nauseous that I sometimes had to stop my bike and throw up. I biked along the Potomac River, and there was a particular spot on the path, just after a slight incline, where I regularly lost my cookies. Usually I made it off the bike first, but every once in a while I would convince myself I wasn't actually going to vomit, but would end up throwing up into the wind, and all over my bike. The other bikers would sometimes stop to see if I was okay or just slow down and rubber neck. I was sure everyone thought I was bulimic, but I didn't want to tell my fellow anonymous bike commuters I was pregnant before I had even told my parents, so I left it a mystery.

Luckily, the fog of nausea lifted at the twelve week mark of pregnancy. I suddenly felt great and had loads of energy. I still wasn't showing much, so biking was a breeze through the second trimester. By the third trimester, biking was by far the most comfortable way for me to get around. It took pressure off of my pelvis, and didn't cause the shooting pains down my leg that sitting or walking did. Despite the physical comfort, though, it was during that third trimester that biking to work became unbearable. As I said, it wasn't because of the biking itself, but instead because of the commentary I would receive from other people. As I biked past the Jefferson Memorial and the Tidal Basin every day, inevitably a few pedestrians would scream things at me, such as "You're endangering your baby!" "That doesn't look safe!" "Think about your baby!" "That's child abuse!" The thing is, I was thinking about my baby. First off, my little fetus was benefiting from my exercise, according to studies.[1] As a result, I was in great shape when it came time for labor, which allowed me to have a carbon-saving natural birth. (Also, I never found any basis for the accusation that biking was more dangerous for my baby than driving or other forms of commuting.) Most importantly, my biking to work during my pregnancy was my way of eliminating pollution from my commute and protecting the planet for my baby. In short, I was doing it for my baby.

I ended up biking until I was eight months pregnant, when I could no longer deal with the stress of being yelled at by onlookers. At that point, I caved and switched to public transportation. As I crammed into a Metro where people were packed tight like sardines in a can, intermittently elbowing my stomach and telling me I really shouldn't be riding the Metro in my condition, I realized that I would be criticized for whatever method of commuting I chose at that point. I worked mostly from home for the final few weeks of my pregnancy.

As I reflected on this experience later on, I realized that I had done the wrong thing by caving in to the strangers who had bullied me into not biking. I was entering a stage of my life where, because of my baby, I was going to draw much more attention in public. Like it or not, I would be now be under attack by people whose views of "safety" were often formed by corporations trying to sell them unhealthy things (car companies, oil companies, etc.) I knew then that I could no longer give in to the fear mongers. If I did, where would it end? If you give in to the opinions of others and don't bike while pregnant, for example, do you also reject an efficient car for a behemoth SUV (the kind that has such a huge blind spot that it's easy to accidentally hit a child on a bike)? Ultimately, my experience as a pregnant biking woman was like a metaphor for our environmental future. If we are afraid of new clean energy, do we instead cling to the dirty, unhealthy, and dangerous energies of the past, risking the unbearable intensity of climate change impacts like heat waves and heavy downpours? In the end, you have to ask yourself what is scarier: changing your everyday activities in spite of pressure from others, or continuing the same activities that are destroying the planet?

Feeding The Beast: Diet During Pregnancy

The only downside of riding my bike and doing exercise during my pregnancy is that it made me very hungry (and I was pretty hungry even on days when I didn't bike or exercise), which re- quired me to consume extra calories. I felt good, however, that these extra calories were coming from foods like lentils, and other low-carbon dietary choices. It turns out that I am not the only woman who was making similar dietary choices. A recent study in Germany found that men eat the majority of the meat consumed in that country, whereas women have a much more vegetable-based diet. The analysis revealed that if men had the same diet as women, about 15,000 km2 less land would be needed for fodder and cattle, which is about 5 percent of the total land area in Germany. Saving that land for trees, and avoiding the carbon footprint of raising cattle would also mean that total German carbon pollution would be reduced by nearly 6 percent.[2]

This study is just one of many confirming that eating a diet light on dairy and meat is the best way to reduce the carbon footprint of your pregnancy. Unfortunately, women can feel enormous pressure from friends and family to eat meat and dairy products during pregnancy in order to get enough iron and B vitamins. Before I switched to using midwives, my doctor questioned me about whether I was sure that I wanted to maintain a vegetarian diet during pregnancy. My response was to ask her if she had any evidence that it wasn't safe, which she didn't. I was concerned that my doctor would ask such a question without having done any research on the topic, so I did a little research on my own. It turns out that there is no evidence that humans need to consume meat or dairy products during pregnancy, and there is ample evidence that vegetarian mothers produce healthy offspring. For example, the American Dietetic Association updated their position paper on vegetarian diets in 2009 to say that

...appropriately planned vegetarian diets, including total vegetarian or vegan diets, are healthful, nutritionally adequate and may provide health benefits in the prevention and treatment of certain diseases. Well-planned vegetarian diets are appropriate for individuals during all stages of the life-cycle including pregnancy, lactation, infancy, childhood and adolescence and for athletes.[3]

Celebrities like Alicia Silverstone (who was very public about maintaining a vegan diet throughout her pregnancy) have helped pave the way for broader acceptance of low carbon diets during pregnancy. Although my own immediate family in India is not vegetarian, half of the population of the country is, including during pregnancy, and there don't appear to be any widespread fertility issues. A balanced diet that includes whole grains, fruits, vegetables, nuts, lentils, fortified cereal, tofu, etc., can provide sufficient nutrition during your pregnancy, and is much lighter on your carbon footprint than eating meat or diary.

A Low Carbon Meal For Pregnancy

One of my favorite meals when I was pregnant was a simple soup and salad. (This recipe could easily be made vegan by omitting the egg and yogurt.)

Spinach, Arugula, or other leafy greens

Corn

Hard Boiled Egg (from a farm share or farmer's market)

Sunflower seeds or chick peas

Tofu cubes

Seasonal roasted vegetables (asparagus or winter root vegetables)

Dried Fruit (raisins, chopped prunes, dried cranberries, etc.)

Ginger salad dressing

For the soup, I cubed a butternut or acorn squash and threw it in a crock pot or pressure cooker with some vegetable broth, a cinnamon stick, a few balls of all-spice, and a pinch of nutmeg. When it was done, I removed the spices that were floating in the soup, and blended it. I would eat the whole thing with a piece of whole grain bread and a dollop of locally produced yogurt.

The Birth Of Your Child

A 2009 article in the *Journal of the American Medical Association* estimated that the United States health care system produces a whopping 8 percent of our country's greenhouse gas pollution, compared to the United Kingdom, where the National Health Service accounts for just 3 percent. In the US, the carbon cost of healthcare is about 325 g per dollar, coming largely from hospitals and the use of pharmaceuticals. This estimate includes the lifecycle carbon emissions of prescription drugs, the carbon emissions from all administrative and insurance-related work, the electricity used by hospitals, and durable and disposable hospital equipment.[4]

It is not surprising then, to learn that hospitals in this country are a major contributor to the carbon footprint of pregnancy and birth, as the majority are still in the Stone Age when it comes to low-carbon technologies such as energy efficient lighting and insulated windows. Most do not even have recycling programs for medical materials, despite evidence that reprocessed medical equipment is safe.[5]* In fact, hospitals are the second largest producers of waste in the United

---

*We all know that it is safe to compost food, but is it safe to recycle medical equipment? Researchers from Johns Hopkins published a paper in March 2010 noting that with proper sterilization, recalibration and testing, reuse of equipment is safe. The Government Accountability Office has also confirmed this. A recent study showed that reprocessed medical equipment does not present an increased health risk over new devices. The paper went on to note that by recycling medical products and procuring fewer disposable medical supplies, hospitals could save hundreds of millions of dollars.

States, behind the food industry. When we think about giving birth, the image of a coal-fired power plant belching pollution does not come to mind. And yet, most births in the United States occur in poorly insulated hospitals powered mainly by coal-fired electricity. This isn't initially the fault of the hospital, since coal is the most common source of electricity in the US, but most hospitals don't choose a renewable energy source over coal, and do very little to control how much coal they are using.[6]

Apart from the wasted electricity, giving birth in a hospital also increases your chances of having a Caesarean section. This is relevant for your carbon footprint because a C-section is a major operation, and any major operation has an associated high carbon footprint. Since we know the carbon footprint per dollar spent in the US health care, we can calculate the carbon footprint of different procedures based on their cost.[7] (The website www.howmuchisit.org provides information on the cost of medical procedures.) For my calculations, I'll use the numbers I was given by my health insurance company. Assuming a cost of $15,000 for a C-section, and assuming that the operation is about average in its carbon use, the carbon footprint would be around 5 tons, which is approximately what an average person on the planet uses in an entire year (and one fourth of what the average American uses in a year).[8] By contrast, I was quoted $9,000 for a vaginal birth in a local hospital. If that vaginal birth was also about average in its carbon use, the carbon footprint would be around three tons.[9] Assuming a birth center price tag of around $6,000, the carbon footprint would be around 2 tons, less than half that of a C-section. A number of studies have confirmed the cost-effectiveness of natural birth, though no existing studies make the link to reduced carbon pollution.[10] Based on the back of the envelope calculations presented here, if you want to have a zero carbon footprint baby for the first year, a C-section will start you off at a severe disadvantage, and require you to redouble your efforts in other areas of footprint reduction.

The best bet for a low carbon birth then is natural birth, which use as little medication and disposable equipment as possible. In addition to being better for your health and the health of the planet, natural birth also increases your odds of being able to breastfeed, and it avoids C-sections and the associated high footprint pharmaceutical and medical waste costs that come with them. While there are numerous advantages to natural birth, if having one involves long drives across state lines for monthly doctor appointments, it is possible that the carbon footprint of your birth decision would be lower by choosing a hospital birth with a health care provider who has a record of avoiding unnecessary medical interventions. The carbon emissions from driving a long distance, or from a midwife driving to visit you, could far outweigh any carbon budget savings from avoiding hospital waste.

Steps To Avoiding A C-section

1. Choose your health care provider and birth setting carefully. In some hospitals, up to 50 percent of births are C-sections, despite the fact that most experts tell us that less than 10 percent of births medically indicate the need for one.[11] If C-sections are common in the hospital you intend to give birth in, it is more than likely you will end up having one.

2. Educate yourself about the medical procedures that will be suggested during your labor. At every point in the process, ask whether the intervention being proposed is actually necessary. Do your own research so that you can learn as much as possible about these interventions beforehand. "Virtually no pregnant women managed within the conventional medical system escape without having tests, drugs, procedures, or restrictions that studies show offer little or no benefit when used indiscriminately, but which introduce risk," writes Henci Goer, in *The Thinking Woman's Guide to Better Birth*.[12]

3. Stay at home for as long as possible, and move around and change positions. The hospital setting can cause anxiety and stress, and mothers in labor generally do better hobbling around their homes, rather than rushing to the hospital at the first sign of labor. In her book *The Birth Partner*, Penny Simkin notes that, "When the mother is free to move and change positions, she is more comfortable, and her labor may even speed up. She finds positions or movements that feel right to her."[13] Talk to your doctor in advance about when you need to go to the hospital and whether hospital policy will allow you to move around once you arrive.

4. Don't rely on your (or your partner's) ability to stay calm and focused in the middle of labor. Instead, find a doula or midwife who is supportive of your desire to avoid a C-section and other potentially unnecessary procedures. You can locate a doula near you at www.dona.org. Also, ask a doula or midwife which actions will increase your risk of needing a C-section. According to William and Martha Sears, in *The Birth Book*, "Studies have shown that mothers who were supported during their labors had shorter labors... and were less likely to need cesareans..."

The Carbon Footprint Of A Home Birth

Humans have been giving birth long before coal or gas were used for energy, and hopefully, we will be giving birth long after we give up fossil fuels and their associated pollution. If you live in the Unites States, it is likely that in addition to your hospital, your home is also powered by coal, unless you have proactively switched to green power through your utility (you can find out by checking the EPA website at: http://oaspub.epa.gov/powpro/ept_pack.charts). In 2011, coal was by far the largest source of electricity in the US, representing 42 percent of electricity generation. The difference between a hospital that consumes coal and your home, however, is that you can control the carbon footprint of your home.

A home birth requires relatively few materials: old clothes, some clean towels and wash cloths, cord clamps, ties of ribbon, scissors, cleaning supplies, food, and drink. Since most of these materials can be found in the home already, there can be almost zero associated carbon with a home birth. However, home births do have an associated cost in the United States. If a home birth is about average in its carbon use compared to other medical interventions, and if it costs around $3,000, which is the quote I received from a local midwife, the carbon footprint would be around 1 ton, or one fifth that of a C-section and a third that of a hospital birth.

Although the carbon footprint of a home birth can be very low, there are situations where one would not be the lowest carbon footprint option. For example, while the number of home births is increasing, they are still relatively uncommon, which results in some serious carbon footprint costs associated with securing home birth assistance. Midwives often have to travel long distances to visit their clients, and clients often have to travel long distances to visit their midwives. If you spend nine months driving fifty miles a month for prenatal care, the carbon footprint of that driving starts to approach that of a birth center or hospital birth. The best option for parents-to-be who do not have a midwife nearby is to choose a doctor who is committed to natural birth.

In the end, although the kind of birth experience a woman has is not entirely under her control, expectant mothers can improve the odds of a lower carbon footprint birth dramatically with careful preparation during pregnancy, a prenatal care provider who has a record of avoiding Cesarean sections, and a birthing location that has a low rate of C-sections. A low carbon footprint birth can start your child's life off in the right way, and also send a signal to your family and friends about your priorities.

My Birth Story

After several days of false alarms, I woke up at three o'clock on a Saturday morning experiencing strong contractions. The false alarms had taught me to stay at home as long as I possibly could. I listened to my "Hypnobabies" breathing recordings and limped around the house, calling out to my husband every few minutes so that he could note another contraction. I also spoke hourly on the phone to my midwife. By seven that night, when I had to have my husband talk to her because I couldn't, she told me I'd better come to the birth center.

I do like to lower my carbon footprint whenever possible, but taking the bus to the birth center was impossible for me at that point because of my physical and mental state. My husband found a taxi, told the driver I was pregnant, and we were on our way. At one point, while trying to focus on the gentle music and breathing exercises playing through my headphones, I looked up to see that the driver had stopped and was giving directions to a lost woman. My husband was gently trying to interrupt and explain that we didn't have time for this when I suddenly belted out, "GO! NOW! HIT THE ACCELERATOR!" The taxi driver suddenly realized that I was close to having a baby, and did as I commanded.

It was about seven thirty when we got to the birth center. I slowly made my way to the entrance and got through another contraction by resting my palms on the wall and going into a version of the yoga pose Uttanasana, in which my torso was perpendicular to my legs. When I finally got to the birth center, my midwife examined me and discovered that I was fully dilated. She asked if I wanted to get into the bathtub, and told me that I would probably feel better if I did. She told us that while water could slow down contractions, since I was fully dilated and the contractions were coming frequently, the water might help in this case. I followed her advice, and I did, indeed, feel better for a moment. The moment was fleeting, however, and it seemed that it was suddenly time to push. The "pushing" stage seemed to last forever, and I felt like I had forgotten to read about that part in my birthing books. After two hours, not much had happened and no one had seen a head yet. I was starting to feel like I could not take much more of this, so without realizing it, I pushed really hard the next time. Suddenly, my precious little baby popped out, his entire amniotic sac intact, in a little bubble. The sac opened in the water and I heard him cry for the first time. The midwives pulled him up, unwrapped the cord from his neck, rested him on my chest and put a little yellow hat on him. I asked if my husband could hold him, and the midwives pointed out that the baby was actually still attached to me since they hadn't yet cut the umbilical cord. The midwives had my husband take off his shirt, cut the cord and hold on to the baby while they helped me out of the tub and onto the bed.

The room was decorated like a little bed and breakfast, except there were absorbent pads everywhere, oxygen tanks in the closets, and emergency equipment disguised as an armoire in the corner. It was the perfect setting for my birth. No one brought out a disposable epidural kit, and everyone wanted to make sure I would be successful at breastfeeding. It was a simple birth in many ways, with nothing used that did not need to be used. They brought the baby over to me and he started nursing immediately. We laid there for a few minutes, me, my husband, and our new baby, in a state of wonder. He was born at 9:23 pm, about eighteen and a half hours after I had gone into labor.

Then the chaos started with the arrival of our families, who had been waiting in the waiting room a few doors down the hall. All of a sudden, Andrew's mom and stepdad, my parents and my sister, were all in our little room. One of the midwives then came to the bedside to tell us that were going to have to go to the hospital because I had a lot of tearing they couldn't take care of there. They recommended that I nurse until I had to leave to ensure that I wouldn't have problems breastfeeding later on, and so that there would be less bleeding. Instead of a disposable hospital gown, they offered me a cotton nightgown that they said I could bring back in a few months. I knew that many women before me had worn that nightgown and that many women would wear it after me as well.

When I arrived at the hospital, the atmosphere could not have been more different. The first thing they did was ask if I had eaten anything in the past few hours. Yes, I had some pizza after I had my baby, I told them. The nurse frowned and said that they couldn't give me general anesthesia for the stitches then. My midwife asked me if I thought I would be okay with local anesthesia, and I said I was sure I'd be fine. Then another nurse came in and told me that I needed an IV. After poking around on my left arm for a while and failing to insert the IV, I asked her why I needed one at all. She told me that is was for general anesthesia. Oh good, I said. Then I don't need it. I was just told that since I had eaten, I couldn't have any general anesthesia. Nope, she said. That's not how it works. She told me that I had to have the IV anyway, as it was hospital policy. I asked if they were at least going to hydrate me or something using the IV, and she said no because then they would have to give me a catheter, though they would be happy to do that, if I wanted one. Why would I want a catheter, I asked? I didn't even want an IV! There was not a thought given to the wastefulness of using an item that wasn't necessary on a patient who didn't want it.

Luckily my midwife was there to keep me calm through the bureaucracy, and the stitching job. By two in the morning, I had been reunited with my husband and baby. Later, as my parents drove us the few miles back home, I heard the harrowing tale of a woman in labor who had pulled in to the birth center just after we left with the cops on her tail. One officer actually pulled a gun on this woman for speeding through lights. The midwives calmly took care of that situation, too.

The next morning we had a lovely visit from the midwives, who gave us an update on the three other moms who had given birth the night before, checked our baby, answered our questions and promised to come by the next day. They asked if we could give them the name of our son, and we decided on Siddharth. Since he was born in his bag of waters, like the Dalai Lama was supposedly, we thought it would be fitting if we gave him one of the names for Buddha.

Education

Ultimately, providing women with the best health education and care is not only good for them, but also for the planet; and it is especially important in an age when human actions are dramatically changing the environment. When a woman has a positive birth experience, is given the tools to breastfeed, healthier children are the result, and there is often less pressure to have additional children. Educated women are also more likely to be exposed to information about birth control options, resulting in empowered mothers who have the number of children they want, and no more. This tends to have a positive effect on the environment because it results in slower population growth, and less consumption of fossil fuels.

When I was a Peace Corps volunteer in Morocco, one of the women I became friendly with was a thirty-something mother of two school-age children. She lived in the same village she had grown up in, and imagined that she would have the same kind of life her mother—who had worked hard her whole life and died tragically giving birth to her fourth child—had had. This woman told me that the day she learned she could get access to free birth control was the day she realized that her life could be different than that of her mother. And indeed, it was different. She had two children whom she loved to pieces, and access to excellent health services for women in the village. While the relationship between population and pollution is not that simple, the story of my friend shows that no matter where you live, access to compassionate and woman-centered maternal healthcare is critical on a planet with a changing climate.

It may sound hokey, but I believe that the way that you start your baby's life sets the tone for the life that follows. Starting off your pregnancy and birth experience with the lowest carbon footprint means that the decisions you make in the ensuing years are more likely to also follow that path. For us, it also set the tone for our loved ones, and started to socialize the idea that we were raising our baby in a different way. Throughout my pregnancy, we were able to share with our family the compelling evidence that fewer interventions are better, not worse for a healthy birth. We were also able to convince ourselves that if we got through pregnancy and birth without a car, for example, we could certainly raise a child without one. We successfully started our journey as parents in the same way that we planned to parent our child, and in a manner that was totally consistent with our values. As a result, we positioned ourselves to succeed in lowering our carbon footprint even in a year that was different from any other of our lives.

Zero Footprint Options

Staying healthy during pregnancy and striving for a natural birth are critical actions to take if you aspire to have a zero carbon footprint baby. Choose a balanced, low-carbon footprint diet. Bike, walk, or use public transportation to get to prenatal care, and prepare yourself for a natural birth in order to maximize the chances of avoiding a series of cascading carbon-intensive birth interventions. Surgery is very expensive, both in economic and environmental terms. The lowest carbon footprint option of home birth is around one ton of carbon, whereas the highest carbon footprint birth would be a C-section, which has a carbon footprint of five or more tons.

3. All That Baby Gear

"You can't have everything... where would you put it?"—Steven Wright

At birth, the average baby is 20 inches long, and weighs about 7.5 pounds. But if you take your cues from society, a seven and a half pound baby needs at least ten times its body weight in stuff in order to survive. For example, the bestselling book *Baby Bargains* tries to narrow down the list of things your tiny baby will need. "Follow all the tips in this book, and we estimate the first year will cost you $4149. Yes, that's a savings of $2891!" the authors tell us, implying that most people spend $7040 on just the bare necessities for their newborn.[1] And that estimate does not even include toys, a $21 billion dollar industry.[2] While the American obsession with consumption is not limited to babies, it does seem to go into overdrive where birth is concerned. The problem with baby stuff is the same problem with all stuff—it is mostly produced using non-renewable resources, built to last for a short amount of time, and rarely recycled when its lifetime ends. The other problem with baby stuff is that when you accumulate too much of it, you need somewhere to put it.

It is difficult to assess the precise amount of carbon pollution from all this recommended consumption because the source of the pollution is the actual production process for making all these products, which can be hard to determine. As a very rough calculation on toys, however, we could assume that in the first year, most parents buy about 20 pounds of plastic, which would result in about 70 pounds of carbon pollution. Assuming about 20 board books or toys with a similar carbon footprint, that's another 47 pounds of carbon pollution.[3] Add another 133 pounds from onesies, and you have around 250 pounds of carbon pollution (0.1 ton) for your tiny baby[4] In the worst case scenario, all this baby stuff gets used (if at all) for a few months, and is then put into boxes that parents either plan on donating, or using for a second child. If parents don't get rid of this stuff quickly—and many new parents are too busy or frazzled to quickly get rid of stuff their baby no longer needs—it gets put into a truck and moved to a storage unit or a newer, bigger house. Since a bigger house needs more energy to heat, cool, and run, your carbon footprint soars in order to accommodate things that are barely getting any use in the first place.

In this chapter, we will explore the carbon footprint implications of baby gear such as clothes, toys, and carriers, as well as alternatives to the consumption of new items.

Gayle's Consumption Story

Gayle is an events coordinator, who pulls off some of the most beautiful events I have ever seen. She is organized and there is no question that she is a planner. When Gayle was pregnant with her first baby, she and her husband Michael went through all the lists of "essentials" and bought everything the baby books told them to buy. They had a baby registry, a baby shower, and spent months painting and furnishing a nursery and picking out matching mobiles and plush toys. Three years later, their son had outgrown everything—including the décor in his room—and Gayle and Michael had gotten rid of everything that had purchased for their baby, since they had moved and didn't have much storage space in their home.

When Gayle became pregnant with her second child, she was empowered with the knowledge that she did not need many of the things that were advertised so heavily to new parents. She didn't want a baby shower, and knew that her baby daughter wouldn't miss out by not having her nursery set match her changing table, dresser, and crib, and that she wouldn't mind having her diaper changed on the bed, on the floor, or any available surface. For the first six months, the new baby girl slept either in the bed with mom and dad, or in a borrowed portable crib. Gayle also borrowed clothes from a friend with a baby who was a little bit older, and returned batches of clothes every few weeks as her baby girl grew out of them. Gayle and Michael didn't buy any new toys. In the end, they had no regrets about not consuming so much for their second baby. They did, however, wish that they could somehow travel back in time and get back the $4,000 they had spent on their son's nursery set—they could have really used that money a few years later for nursery school!

Too Many Clothes and Collaborative Consumption

New parents are told they will need lots of clothes, and baby showers are seen as an occasion for friends and family to buy those clothes. As a result, more baby clothes are manufactured than our society actually needs.

If you need proof that Americans have too many baby clothes, just consider that clothes for babies have almost no resale value. Instructions for local consignment shops and flea markets will tell you that for sizes 0 to 4T, you must bundle clothes into lots of multiple articles and price them very low in order to sell. The pricing guidelines for Wee-Sale, a popular traveling Maryland children's consignment market, instruct sellers to charge very little for baby clothes. According to their website, "If you have 0-2T they MUST be priced on the lower end, regardless of brand!!!"[5] Clothes for older children can be sold at three times the price of infant clothes. This reflects simple economics of supply and demand: the supply of baby clothes is too high, so the price at which you can sell them is very low.

Part of this problem is because, before having a baby, it is easy to feel like you need a lot of clothes. But, when purchasing clothes for your baby, consider how many weeks your son or daughter will be under 10 pounds, how many weeks they will be between 10 and 20 pounds (and in which seasons), and you will quickly realize how short a useful lifespan most baby clothes have. You will need most newborn clothes for very little time, and your baby will likely wear any given item only a handful of times. Most parents are shocked to realize that some of the adorable baby clothes they received as gifts or bought only fit their child once before he or she outgrows them. If you're not paying careful attention, you may even miss the window of squeezing your baby into some of their outfits. Despite this, many parents and their friends and family feel the need to buy piles of clothes for their baby.

Unfortunately, this baby-related consumption is both expensive and not good for our carbon footprints. For example, if you just count the cotton in the onesies that most babies wear, you're talking about 130 pounds of CO_2.[6] Luckily, there is an easy way to eliminate this carbon footprint—simply buy nothing new and ask others to only give you pre-loved items. There are also some niche products available for babies that are sewn from salvaged or recycled fabrics, which is a great option if you just cannot get your loved ones to purchase used baby clothes. My sister got my son a "Cotton Monster" stuffed animal that is made from old garments, and sold at local craft markets.

In 2010, *Time Magazine* named "Collaborative Consumption" as one of the ten ideas that will change the world. The concept is simple: rather than own items yourself, businesses can enable you to share, swap, barter, trade, or rent access to what you need. The most commonly cited example is car sharing, which allows customers to use cars on an hourly basis, as an alternative to car ownership. Collaborative Consumption is the perfect model for baby things. Since babies grow and develop so quickly in the first year of their lives, nearly everything that you buy for them is only useful for one to two months. Economic models based on collaborative consumption would allow parents to use the baby items they need for the time they need it, rather than own them past their usefulness date. Companies like Craigslist and Ebay enable collaborative consumption across a range of items—just give yourself some time to allow for slower, more efficient, shipping. Recently a few companies, like ThredUp and Diaperswappers have emerged that cater directly to the needs of parents of babies. They are simple to use and are a great way to reduce your carbon footprint. Sellers simply bag or box all the baby clothes that no longer fit and post them online. Buyers can search by gender, season, and age, and select the boxes of items that they need.

Toys

For most of the first year of your baby's life, you (the baby's parents) are the best toy for them. They stare at your eyes and watch your every move. Not only is your presence free, but it is about as low consumption as it gets. Unfortunately, there is money to be made from convincing you otherwise, and so mountains of crib mobiles, rattles, activity centers, plush toys, board books, and stacking toys are sold every year in this country—3.6 billion toys annually. While only 4 percent of the world's children are American, they own 40 percent of the world's toys.[7] Parents who do not subscribe to this "culture of toys" often feel guilt over their minimalist ways, asking themselves if their child has what he or she needs to develop properly.

I must say that at the beginning of my son's life, I felt some of this guilt. I saw the mobiles and stuffed animals in other peoples' homes and wondered if my baby needed those toys, too. Then I did a little research, which revealed that low-consumption parents have nothing to worry about. Quite the opposite: Depriving your child of store-bought toys actually nurtures their development by fostering creativity. Psychologist Susan Linn states the problem clearly in her book *Consuming Kids*:

> Play thrives in environments that provide children with safe boundaries, but do not impinge on ability to think or act spontaneously. It is nurtured with opportunities for silence. For children who are flooded continually with stimuli and commands to react, the cost is high. They have fewer opportunities to initiate action or influence the world they inhabit, and less chance to exercise the essential human trait of creativity.[8]

For an older baby, a toy car can be a toy car and nothing else, whereas a small cardboard box can be opened and shut for fun, and can go from being a car to a house to a phone. Unfortunately, babies today are unlikely to be attracted to that sort of creative play because they are bombarded with media characters, screens, and toys that have a fixed shape and purpose. The most extreme example of a baby scam is the "Baby Einstein" video series that tries to convince parents that by buying videos and sitting their babies in front of a television, those infants will turn out smarter. In fact, exactly the opposite is true, as "screen time" for children under the age of two can result in obesity later on in life, as well as behavioral, sleep, and academic problems.[9] It also causes more carbon pollution than just the immediate pollution associated with buying the video, as the Department of Energy has found that energy use and carbon pollution from televisions and related gadgets is increasing dramatically.[10]

Even less extreme examples of baby toys can be harmful. By the age of six months, babies who watch television can form mental images of corporate logos, mascots, and characters, and, as a result, many children request specific brands and characters from the moment they speak.[11] Despite our low-consumption ways, our son was talking about Elmo before he knew the names of most of our family members, as we had been given a hand-me-down cup and two hand me down books with Elmo's image on them, and that was enough to start an obsession. Before he had reached the age of one, Siddharth was pointing at things at the grocery store and asking for any item that carried Elmo—a licensed character that we did not intentionally introduce to him. I assume that this reaction from infants is exactly what the marketers envisioned when they put Elmo's face on everything from cups to books.

Ten Best Toys For Babies

In their first few months, babies do not need, or even notice, toys—they just need you! Once they can sit up, a few toys can be fun for them. Here were our baby's favorites, none of which increased our carbon footprint very much, if at all:

1. Sticks

2. Rocks (Bigger than a ping pong ball, so it's not a choking hazard)

3. Leaves (Avoid the leaves of house plants, which can be toxic)

4. Cardboard box to sit in

5. Board book (can be used or from the library)

6. Recycling items (old cups, newspapers, magazines, etc.)

7. String, yarn, rope

8. Dirt (No dog poop in the dirt, please, but garden variety dirt is pretty safe)

9. Spoon (a wooden spatula or serving spoon is highly entertaining)

10. Anything he saw us paying attention to (cell phone, wallet, credit card)

Feeding Supplies

Like clothes, most feeding supplies for your newborn can be found used. However, they are not as widely traded as clothing, so planning in advance or even better, having a friend with an older baby, can be helpful. Right after Siddharth was born, I was able to borrow a used breastfeeding pillow, used glass bottles (with used slow flow nipples), and used breast pumps and parts from my friend Stacey. A big advantage of borrowing these items was that she could tell me and my husband what they were and why we needed them. When we first brought the breast pump into the house, we were perplexed. Fortunately, Stacey was able show us the difference between a valve, a membrane, and a breast shield. (The "My Breast Friend" pillow, on the other hand, was pretty intuitive.) Once our son was a few months old, Andrew joked that some men knew how to clean and load guns quickly, but that no one could wash and assemble pump parts as fast as he could.

If you don't have a friend to borrow from, breast pumps and parts can be rented from your local hospital or breast feeding center. Hospital grade pumps are expensive to buy, but relatively affordable to rent; non-hospital grade pumps are usually not made for multiple users, and cannot be opened or cleaned. There is at least one non-hospital grade pump that is made for multiple users, however, by Hygeia. I have found quite a lot of information on Hygeia on social media and from friends who are enthusiasts of its pump. Hygeia also has a program that allows mothers to refurbish their pumps and share them with one another. After the first six months, as your baby starts to eat solids, you'll need different kinds of supplies, such as baby spoons and a high chair. While you can easily survive without a high chair, they are relatively easy to borrow from a friend or find used at a consignment shop.

The Spoon

The moment when Siddharth was ready to eat solids came upon us rather suddenly. One day, we realized we were having to hide from him in order to eat, and decided to give him some food in a spoon. But we didn't have a baby spoon and hadn't really anticipated wanting one. As if by divine intervention, that same day my husband had found a baby spoon in the street. We washed and sterilized it, then decided to use it to give our baby his first solid food. After feeding him some sweet potato, I put him to bed and blogged about my found spoon. I felt pretty lucky that we found what we needed with so little effort.

About a month later, we got a package in the mail from my sister in-law containing a bunch of used spoons. A week after that, our baby sitter brought over two more spoons. At first I didn't make the connection, but I later realized that everyone was giving me spoons because of my blog post. I decided that, from then on, I would take advantage of my generous friends and post on Facebook whenever I needed something. Soon, I was rolling in "new to me" collections of used cloth diapers, blankets, and crib sheets. In the next chapter I explore the carbon footprint of cloth diapers more deeply, but one aspect of their carbon footprint comes from the manufacturing of new diapers. Because of that, I was always on the lookout for used cloth diapers. When my son grew out of the last of the diapers I had borrowed from a friend, I posted on Facebook that I needed cloth diapers for older babies. A friend from high school, Elisha, saw the post. We hadn't seen each other in nearly twenty years, but she was still happy to send me a huge bag of cloth diapers she had used on her sons, in order to get them out of her house. Her generosity meant that no more cotton needed to be grown in order for my baby to wear cloth diapers. That in turn meant a lower carbon footprint because I was able to avoid the pollution involved with cultivating and processing cotton for new diapers.

What if Everyone Did This? Wouldn't the Economy Collapse?

While people could complain about all of the low-carbon options in this book on the grounds that it's not good for the economy to refrain from buying things, the real question is, "Can we afford to keep producing all this stuff and throwing it away?" The answer to that question is clearly "no." Simply put, we are currently using resources at a faster rate than the planet can replenish them. The raw materials that go into our baby clothes and toys simply cannot be produced at the rate that we are currently consuming them. If everyone were to consume the way that Americans do, we would need four planets to produce the necessary raw materials.[12] For ecological reasons alone, we need to stop consuming at our current rate.

The economics can work too, as new models like collaborative consumption show that society can function with fewer things. Recycling services and recycled products will do well in the new, low-carbon economy, as will service-oriented businesses that minimize waste. So, to answer the question, if everyone were living this way, no, the economy would not collapse, it would just transform into one that only uses materials at the rate that the Earth can produce those materials.

What Do You Really Need? (It depends on how you define "need")

Every baby book I ready while I was pregnant listed two or three pages of gear that I would absolutely need in order to take care of my baby. Having never been a parent, it was difficult to differentiate between items that were a scam and items that would actually make my life easier. To try and figure out what to do, I surveyed the most minimalist parents I knew, and came up with a list of ten items that are necessary for taking care of a new baby. All of these items can be purchased or borrowed in a pre-loved condition:

1. Car seat, to get home from the hospital/birth center or if you need a car to get around. (Even if you do not have a car, in

the US, all hospitals or birth centers require that you own a car seat.)

2. Carrier for infant (I borrowed a Moby Wrap, and had a hand me down Baby Bjorn. After the first six months, I got a used stroller.)

3. Bouncy chair or other surface (to sleep in during the day/ hang out in.)

4. Clothes and burp cloths (This is the easiest thing to borrow from others. If you can't beg or borrow one, try getting a box or bundle from thredup.com, kidsstuffsale.com, Ebay, Craigslist, etc.)

5. Thermometer (This is a hard item to find used, but borrowing might be an option.)

6. Nail clippers/file (You can also bite their little nails once they get long enough.)

7. Diapers (Unless you practice elimination communication, which is potty training without a diaper.)

8. A breast pump (if you are returning to work outside the home, or have concerns about low milk supply).

9. Eight glass 4 oz bottles (you can pump straight into these and freeze them for later use).

10. A crib and mattress (if you decide not to co-sleep).

Zero Footprint Options

Thirty percent of the carbon footprint of China can be attributed to the manufacturing of products for other countries' consumption.[13] Manufacturing things for babies produces carbon pollution. However, buying new gear for a baby is completely unnecessary in today's society, where you can always find used items. To eliminate this part of your carbon footprint, only buy used or 100 percent recycled items, take advantage of collaborative consumption, and realize that you are the only thing that your baby truly needs to be happy. The 3.6 billion toys that are purchased every year are not good for our children, or the environment. Baby toys, baby clothes, and baby gear are all marketed by companies that want you to believe that those things will help you and help your baby develop. They are plastered with images that your baby will start to recognize from infancy, so that when your infant becomes a toddler, they will ask you to buy the items that have been marketed to them since their birth. Before you know it, your house can seem too small for all of the stuff that goes along with your tiny baby. The truth is that your baby doesn't need most of that stuff. Your baby just wants to be held, to stare into your face, and to feel your warmth. As a parent, it is your job to feed your baby and keep your baby warm, dry and safe. It is also your job as a parent to leave your child a habitable planet that is not devastated by climate change. These two jobs are not in contradiction. Taking care of a baby requires a lot of love and patience, but not a lot of "things."

4. Are Cloth Diapers A "Clothian" Bargain?

"Diaper backwards spells repaid. Think about it."—Marshall McLuhan

In 1961, Proctor & Gamble introduced Pampers, a single-use diaper that could be tossed into the trash instead of washed, to the world. This invention revolutionized the way people changed their children, and within thirty years, over 90 percent of babies in the United States were using disposable diapers, and the word "Pampers" had become synonymous with "diapers."[1] Along with the rise of the disposable diaper, however, has come a predictable increase in landfill waste. Today, diapers account for about 2 percent of all landfill waste, as well as causing millions of pounds of guilt that weigh heavily on the shoulders of new parents.[2] But are disposable diapers really an inferior alternative to old-fashioned cloth diapers from a carbon footprint perspective, particularly since cloth diapers are generally made of relatively carbon-intensive cotton and have to be washed, dried, and transported?

In this chapter, I will examine the impact of diapering on climate change and carbon footprints, focusing on three options: cloth, disposable, and diaper-free. Unlike other general household choices, there is no way for diapering to play a positive role in addressing climate change and reducing consumption. When you are preparing a room for your baby you can decide to insulate with better curtains and actually reduce your carbon footprint below what is was before your baby was born. Similarly, when you are deciding where to live, you can choose a home that is more transit-oriented, which will allow you to use a car less than you did before becoming a parent. But when you are diapering, you have no choice but to use more energy than you did before you had a child. As you will see in this chapter, though, the impact of diapers is relatively small and can even be eliminated.

Elimination Communication

My husband and I happened to be visiting my cousin and his wife in India when their twin daughters were three months old. At the time, we were not even thinking about having children of our own and approached our interactions with my cousin's family with the detached interest of outside observers. We watched how the twins ate the same food the adults were eating, only mashed; slept only when coerced to do so by vigorous bouncing and reassuring; and—most astoundingly—used the toilet to go to the bathroom. That's right: these three-month-old babies did not use diapers.

This observation turned the traditional "cloth vs. disposable" debate on its head for me. Years earlier, I had realized that the old "paper or plastic" debate at the grocery store was a false choice, and that the real answer was a reusable bag. Now, I had discovered a similar "third way" of thinking with regards to diapers. Thus, when I became pregnant with my son a few years later, I started asking my Indian relatives how to do the whole diaperless thing. Unfortunately, most of the answers were more confusing than helpful. "It's no secret," my cousin's wife in India emailed me. "There's no trick to it. You just take them to the toilet." My mother and her friends, who had raised their babies in the US with disposable diapers, had only vague memories from India of infants without diapers. "You just put a bowl under them as newborns when they go to the bathroom," one friend told me.

Eventually, I discovered a movement of parents in the US and Canada who practiced diaperless baby rearing, a process known as "elimination communication."[3] The philosophy behind elimination communication is that, from birth, babies naturally prefer to avoid soiling themselves, and it is possible to help them do so by teaching them cues for peeing and pooping and by getting to know their schedule. Elimination communication can be started at any age, though you shouldn't wait too long, as it is easier to begin implementing before your baby is actively moving around. There are three basic steps to the process:

Step 1 (optional). Diaperless time. Set aside some time for your baby to lie on a water resistant surface without a diaper on so that you can figure out when he or she pees or poops.

Step 2. Choose a sound as a "cue," and as soon as you see your baby going to the bathroom, make that noise. I used "pssss" for peeing and "ugh" for pooping with my son. Make this noise any time your baby pees or poops, regardless of whether it is in a diaper, in the bathtub, on the changing table, or all over your clothes.

Step 3. Notice when your baby normally pees and poops (e.g. right after feeding, or when he or she gets home from being outside). During these times, hold your baby over a small baby toilet, an actual toilet, or a small bowl set aside for this purpose. Don't stress out about catching every pee and poop, just celebrate the ones you do manage to catch. The idea is that you will have more catches and fewer misses once your baby has fewer and more predictable bowel movements at around 3 to 4 months of age. By then, your baby will pee and poop when you put them on the toilet, though the poops can usually be caught more reliably. Of course, there will be some misses when your baby is sick, but believe it or not, you will spend much less time in physical contact with poop using elimination communication than you would with a diaper. When you practice elimination communication, the poop goes straight into the toilet, so you don't have any explosions or leaks.

Of course, implementing the diaperless baby plan is not as easy as it sounds. My son was born in October, and as winter came and the weather got colder, I had a hard time leaving him without a diaper for hours, as is recommended so that babies can learn to associate going to the bathroom with toilets. Also, I didn't have a stable of mother's helpers on hand to help with the baby as my cousin did in India. In addition, working my job left me too overwhelmed at times to practice elimination communication with my son every day. Despite these obstacles, I discovered that it wasn't too difficult to catch his morning poop in the toilet, and that I could almost always elicit peeing by taking him to the toilet. Part-time elimination communication was possible and practical for our family!

The Carbon Footprint Of The Diaperless Baby

Not surprisingly, diaperless baby rearing has by far the lowest footprint of all diapering options. While there are no studies specifically assessing the carbon impact of this practice, the only two pollution causing processes associated with diaperless baby rearing are additional laundry when your child misses the toilet, and additional toilet flushing when there are catches. The additional laundry is minimal compared to your total household laundry, however, so there likely isn't any increased electricity usage since there aren't extra loads of laundry to do, unlike with cloth diapering.

Also, anyone who is serious enough to attempt diaperless child rearing is probably not flushing after the baby pees and only flushing after poops. Assuming an efficient toilet with 1 to 2 gallons per flush, we can estimate that an additional ten gallons of water would be required daily on average for the first year of the baby's life, with an associated 0.004 lb. of CO_2 per gallon.[4] That's less than fifteen pounds of carbon per year, which is a mere rounding error on most people's carbon footprint.

Our Cloth Diaper Story

Since I was returning to a job outside the home and had to rely on others who were not as well versed on elimination communication as I was, I realized that I was not going to be able to go completely diaperless with my son. I was going to need a backup plan. After carefully researching the carbon footprint of cloth and disposable diapers, I decided that home-laundered cloth diapers were the best choice for the environment. I thought that would be the end of the story, but then I actually tried to procure some diapers, and fell into the bewildering world of cloth diaperers (aka CDers).

The world of CDing is a subculture unto itself, and only when I started researching the topic did I realize what a large subculture it is. My first online search on the topic session lasted four hours, and at the end of it, I was more confused about what diapers to get than before I started. There were no cloth diaper stores where I lived, and the amount of jargon and the number of acronyms on the websites I encountered made the simple idea of wrapping a baby in cloth seem bewildering (See Cloth Diaper Acronym and Jargon Decoder). I decided that as a smart woman who spoke many languages, I was going to have to do the same thing I had done many times before: namely, fully immerse myself in the new language of CDing.

I joined my local email listserv for the cloth diapering community (DCCDers) and lurked on the site hoping to absorb some wisdom. It took me about three months to figure it all out, which was a little longer than it had taken me to become confident speaking Spanish, but a little less time than it took me to learn Arabic. Not bad, but no cakewalk, either. In retrospect, I should have sent a note out to everyone I knew and just asked for help from friends who had used cloth diapers. At the time, though, I didn't know that I knew so many people who used cloth diapers, so it didn't occur to me to ask. One friend who had a

CDing mentor told me that it only took her one week to figure it all out, which made me realize that I wasted a lot of time by not asking for assistance.

Compared to the chore of figuring out which diapers to use, actually using cloth diapers turned out to be a breeze. We purchased used diapers off Craigslist, and a friend lent us diaper covers to last us through the first three months. The diapers were tiny, so we only had to add one load of laundry per week. During the week, we just threw the diapers in a hamper with a liner (luckily, our newborn baby's poop and pee didn't smell, as is generally the case until solids or formula is introduced). We washed them in cold water with a natural dye-free soap (we used Nellie's laundry soda from Crate and Barrel). Line drying the diapers outside in the sun got them completely clean, though during the winter months they also dried very quickly on the line indoors.

Cloth Diaper Acronym And Jargon Decoder

Cloth diapers have come a long way since the days of diaper pins, and nowadays almost no one uses those scary pins next to their newborns' skin. Overall, there are a few basic types of cloth diapering systems:

Prefolds with diaper covers and optional snappi closure By far the cheapest option, this is what we used. Basically, a prefold is a rectangular piece of fabric that you fold into the shape of a diaper (It really threw me for a loop that the prefolds were the diapers you had to fold). Snappis are the y-shaped fasteners that are used instead of pins. They have little plastic teeth shaped like the clips that hold an Ace bandage together that you might wrap around your ankle or wrist. The diaper cover is a water proof or water resistant shell that goes over the prefold and is in the shape of a disposable diaper and is held together using a Velcro-type fastening system.

Fitted diapers with diaper covers

Fitted diapers are absorbent cloths in the shape of a diaper with snaps or Velcro that fasten on to your baby. Since the diapers get wet, you still need a water proof diaper cover to go over the fitted diaper.

All in Ones (AIOs)

All in Ones are the easiest cloth diaper option. They come in the same shape as disposable diapers and are fastened either with snaps or Velcro. The part of the diaper that touches the baby is made of felt or a similar material so that moisture is whisked away from the rear end. They are just as simple as disposable diapers to use. The downside is that they are more expensive than prefolds (though still less than disposables over the lifetime of use), and they take a long time to dry, so you need to have 25 to 30 of them on hand.

Pocket diapers

Pocket diapers look like AIO diapers, but they have a pocket that you need to stuff with an absorbent liner. One or two liners usually come with each diaper. The advantage of this model is that the diaper dries much faster on a line since you take the insert out for drying. This system also gives you the flexibility to stuff the diaper more at night when you need greater absorbency and less during the day when you want the diaper to be trimmer to maximize freedom of movement. These are the most popular diapers in my observation, and include brands like BumGenius and FuzziBunz.

Hybrid diapers

A few brands of diapers have emerged that have a disposable insert that can be flushed, composted, or trashed. The exterior of the diaper is reusable and needs to be washed, while the insert can be put in the trash, flushed, or composted.

Cloth Diaper Terms

AIO: All in One diaper

Alplix: A brand of thread and hook fabric fastener, like Velcro

CDers: Cloth diaperers.

Destashing: The act of selling used cloth diapers (e.g. when your infant outgrows the size 0 diapers)

DSQ: Diaper Service Quality, a term used to describe the best prefolds

Gussets: The tapered leg holes of diaper covers

Insert: The cloth fabric put inside a typical pocket diaper. These are usually made of hemp or cotton.

Liner: A disposable or cloth light material that either keeps the baby dry or is used to peel off and flush the poop easily.

OS: One size fits all

Prepping: Pre-washing that is required of some cloth diapers before their first use

PUL: Polyurethane laminated, the waterproof material in many cloth diapers

SAHM: Stay at Home Mom (these moms sometimes sew their own cloth diapers for sale)

Snappi: A Y-shaped fastener that holds prefold diapers onto your baby (replaces the old fashioned sharp diaper pin)

Stash: A person's set of cloth diapers, which usually includes many different types

Stripping: The process by which you remove detergent build-up from diapers

Wet bag: A reusable bag that holds dirty diapers

Cloth vs. Disposable Diaper Carbon Footprint

The first time we used disposable diapers was for a trip to Charlottesville, Virginia when our son was four months old. Because of the number of people who had commented on cloth diapers being harder than disposables, I was expecting things to be easier with the disposable diapers. However, we found that the disposable diapers had a fatal flaw: they didn't actually hold in poop. Now, it's possible that I was doing something wrong, but on multiple occasions we had poop explode out of the back of the diaper and onto our babies' back. This had never happened to us with cloth prefold diapers. When we got back from our trip, I sent a note to a friend who used disposable diapers asking what I was doing wrong. "Nothing," was her answer, "poop explosions are just part of life." After that, I never regretted choosing to use cloth diapers.

Poop issues aside, it is difficult to definitively answer the question of whether cloth or disposable diapers are better from a carbon footprint perspective because it all depends on how you wash the cloth diaper, and what's inside the disposable diaper. The carbon costs of disposable diapers are embedded in the diapers themselves, and come from the manufacturing process and transport of the product, while the carbon costs of cloth diapers come mostly from the user's washing and drying practices. One study from Australia showed that home-laundered cloth diapers had the lowest carbon footprint when compared with diaper service-laundered diapers and disposable diapers.[5] However, a UK study found little difference between home-laundered cloth diapers and disposable diapers.[6]

The most widely-cited study is the latter one, conducted by the British Department of the Environment, so it's worth taking a closer look at the results. The study looked at the life cycle impact of both cloth and disposable diapers from manufacturing through the use and disposal of the diapers (i.e. from picking the cotton and manufacturing the plastic to the product breaking down in a landfill). The researchers calculated the carbon costs of cloth diapers to be between 326 and 503 pounds (148 and 228 kg CO_2e /yr), and the carbon costs of disposables to be an average of 485 pounds per year (220 kg). The two main points to take from this are, first, that the annual carbon footprint of diapers is not very high compared to the carbon footprint of most actions, and second, that there is a range of possible carbon footprints for cloth diapers, which is the result of differing user habits. The lower footprint assumes that the diapers are used on more than one baby, line dried, and washed in full loads in cool water in a high-efficiency washer. The higher end footprint assumes only some line drying, less than full loads and average efficiency appliances.

The UK study has been widely criticized by cloth diapering enthusiasts for a host of reasons. One, the study looked at a number of scenarios for cloth diapers, but even the most environmentally friendly scenario assumed that the diapers were only used on two children. In fact, most families using cloth diapers use some amount of used diapers, and generally reuse or sell their diapers, as cloth diapers keep their value in a way that almost no product on the market does. (A quick look on Craigslist and Ebay shows that cloth diapers lose less than a third of their value even after many months of use on a single baby.) The study also assumed more diaper changes for cloth diapers than for disposable, which resulted in cloth diapers having a larger footprint. The study also did not look at the costs of traveling to the store at regular intervals to procure disposable diapers, nor the energy use of retail stores. The researchers also claimed that the age of toilet training did not differ between cloth and disposable diapers, when many argue that babies in cloth diapers get out of diapers earlier.

What Cloth Diaperers Can Do To Reduce Their Carbon Footprint

Unlike users of disposable diapers, those who choose to use cloth diapers, and can launder at home, have a lot of control over their carbon footprint. For example, by washing the diapers in hot water multiple times and using a dryer for every load, the carbon footprint of someone using cloth diapers can be greater than that of a person using disposable diapers. On the other hand, if cloth diaperers take the following steps, their carbon footprint can be significantly less than that of a person using disposables:

1. Skip the diaper service or use one that delivers via public transportation

2. Line dry the diapers instead of using a dryer. This can be done on a small rack inside your home, if you don't have outdoor space.

3. Use the most energy and water efficient appliances on the market

4. Use cold water or a solar water heating system

5. Wash full loads, to reduce the number of loads of laundry

6. Use the slimmest/smallest possible diapers so that many can be washed at once

7. Buy used cloth diapers. Used cloth diapers can be found on Craigslist, Diaperswappers, and other websites where people share used items.

8. Don't drive to pick-up your diapers; use public transit or shop online and have them mailed to you. If you can find a local person selling used diapers on Craigslist, it is preferable to use public transportation to pick those up, rather than having to drive to get them, or having them shipped.

9. Install or purchase renewable energy if you launder at home

10. Use fewer diapers by practicing elimination communication

Engaging in all of the above practices will essentially limit the carbon footprint of cloth diapers to just the water used for laundering. The embedded carbon will be reduced by only using used diapers, and the carbon footprint from electricity will be eliminated by installing renewable energy at your home. Assuming two loads of laundry per week, this will result in the carbon footprint of cloth diapering being only sixteen pounds of carbon per year. Not everyone has these options, though. In New York City, for example, there are only two cloth diaper services and many families are reliant on a local laundromat. If that is your situation, remember that the electricity used to dry the diapers is the number one reason that the carbon footprint of cloth diapers rivals that of disposables. Are there times when you can dry your diapers at home, even if you use the laundromat for washing? Would the laundromat be willing to wash and line dry the diapers for you? If none of that is possible, remember that the carbon footprint of cloth diapers is not appreciably higher than that of a disposable diaper if you have to use a clothes dryer (0.23 tons for cloth vs. 0.22 tons for disposables). The environmental benefit of cloth diapering, if you must use a driving diaper service or a clothes' dryer, is that you won't be haunted by images of landfills full of your diapers for decades to come.

Mix And Match Diapering

Many parents opt for a combination of diapering methods at different times. For example, parents may chose not to use a diaper service when their babies are only producing water-soluble breast milk poop, but find that later on they need some help with the laundry when their child starts eating more and varied foods. Or the opposite could happen, where parents start out with a diaper service and later realize that it is not so difficult to home launder. Similarly, many parents use a mix of cloth and disposable diapers, using disposable diapers when they are out of the house or traveling, cloth when they are home. Some parents use disposable at night and cloth during the day when the baby is awake and can alert them to when she's just peed or pooped.

Additionally, most day care providers, and some grandparents, refuse to use cloth diapers, so parents are sometimes forced to use disposable diapers in those situations. We were lucky, as our care providers were always willing to use cloth diapers (after a short tutorial) as long as we dealt with any clean up issues. However, we did have to use disposable wipes with one care provider who was willing to go along with us on the diapers, but found the wipes to be a step too far. Regardless of what mix you chose, the principles required to lower your carbon footprint remain the same: use diapers for less time and use as little electricity and gasoline as possible as part of your diapering routine.

Mary's Disposable Diaper To Diaperless Story

Though Mary had read about elimination communication and diaperless babies during her pregnancy, the first months of motherhood were so overwhelming that she didn't feel she had time to use the bathroom regularly herself, much less take her baby to the toilet. However, she wasn't comfortable using regular disposable diapers because of her concerns about the toxic materials used in their production. After considering the options, she decided to go with a bleach-free diaper from Seventh Generation. These were more expensive than cloth diapers or regular disposables, and she was on a tight budget, but it was what she was comfortable putting on her baby.

Mary was in the final week of her maternity leave when she started to notice that her son was having more regular bowel movements. He was four months old and seemed to go to the bathroom three times a day, about five minutes after feeding. She started to hold him over the toilet at those times, and miraculously, he went almost immediately. She also reminded herself to cue him each time he went. As a result, she saved three diapers per day that week, plus wipes, which more than cut in half her diaper usage. (In the spirit of making conversation, Mary told her child care provider what she had been doing. Her nanny was African and did not find it odd at all that a baby would go to the bathroom in a toilet when cued to do so.)

Mary's first day back to work was a difficult one for her. She was running around, trying to get back into the swing of her job while pumping breast milk, and worrying about how things were going at home. Had she left enough milk for her son? How would he adjust to having to wearing a diaper again? In the middle of the day, she heard her cell phone buzz and knew it was her nanny since she had set a special ring tone for those calls. Mary rushed out of a meeting and grabbed her phone, worried that it was an emergency. Her fears turned to smiles when she opened a text message to find a tiny image of poop in a potty!

Although there were both good and bad days for the next few months, Mary and her nanny were able to catch many of her son's poops in the toilet. It was less messy, cheaper, and better for the environment. And the best part was that her son seemed to have a real sense of accomplishment after going in the toilet.

Toilet Training

Since going diaperless is the most environmentally-friendly option, it is worth exploring further the best methods for weaning your baby off diapers during their first year. While books on elimination communication are full of adorable little toddlers who never use diapers and make the sign for potty even before they can say the word, that wasn't how it worked for us. When Siddharth turned one, he started walking, and immediately started walking away from the potty. He wasn't verbal enough yet for me to be able to decipher why he was walking away, but the message was clear—he was done using the potty. After a year of him using the potty regularly when we were home with him, we were back to square one on the toilet training front.

We talked to many different friends, trying to find the right method to get him interested in the toilet again. Some recommended sticker charts as an incentive, but Siddharth showed no interest in stickers. Others swore by the "three day method" where you stay close to your child for three days and run them over to the potty any time they start to go. Other people felt strongly that you just should wait for the child to express interest. In short, we found the world of potty training to be almost as controversial as the world of baby sleep and sleep training. As with the question of how you should get your baby to sleep, everyone has an opinion about toilet training.

Eventually, we decided to go along with our son's "potty strike," as it is called in elimination communication circles, and went back to full-time cloth diapering, until we finally switched to underpants when he turned two. Our personal experience was that using cloth diapers did seem to make our final move to using the toilet a bit easier, since our son was already aware of when he peed, and that seemed to make it simpler to explain the rest. Unfortunately, there is mixed evidence on the question of whether cloth-diapered babies get out of their diapers faster than ones who use disposables. Assuming that there is a correlation between cloth diapers and early potty training, the relationship may or may not be causative. In other words, cloth diapers may actually cause early potty training because babies can feel when they are wet or soiled and do not like the sensation, and hence prefer a toilet. On the other hand, the relationship may be correlative, which means that parents that choose to use cloth diapers are the type of parents who try to potty train as quickly as possible, or practice some of the elements of elimination communication. It also could be that for some parents, using disposable diapers for a short period of time allows them to focus on elimination communication and getting toilet trained more quickly.

Kristine's Story

When Kristine's son Quintin was born, she knew she wanted to breastfeed him for the first year of his life. So, when he was four months old, she started attending a local La Leche League group. That was where she first saw cloth diapers. Although Kristine was interested in using them, her husband, Corey, scoffed that the effort wasn't worth the time, energy and cost needed to wash them. Since Kristine was already feeling overwhelmed at the thought of returning to work in a few months, she didn't argue with her husband or do any further research. She assumed that cloth diapering was something stay-at-home mothers did, mothers who had the time to be "crunchy."

When Kristine had her second baby a few years later, she was a more confident mother and was determined to make the most of her maternity leave. She had already gone "outside the box" and had a home birth, so when cloth diapers crossed her mind again when her daughter was four months old, she eagerly approached the venture. She was also worried about the chemicals in disposable diapers and tired of receiving big boxes of them in the mail that seemed to come with way too much packaging.

Three friends loaned her different types of cloth diapers to try initially, and Kristine quickly realized that cloth diapers were not just simple to wash, but adorable. She immediately started posting pictures of her baby's colorful, fashionable diapers on Facebook. Her husband was still horrified at the idea of washing poop rather than throwing it away, so Kristine promised to change all the diapers, and little by little gave her husband a role in the actual washing of the diapers. Kristine's cloth diapering success showed her that working moms can be crunchy too, and she wondered what other crunchy things she was missing out on. If cloth diapering was so easy, what could she do that might be a bit harder, but would have an even bigger impact? If diapers didn't need to be disposable, what else could she stop throwing away? Was it possible to stop the linear chain of extracting natural resources to make our stuff and then throwing that stuff in the trash? After mastering cloth diapers, Kristine started using cloth breast pads, hand towels, napkins and feminine hygiene products. She even started thinking about whether she'd be willing to give up her gas-guzzling SUV. For Kristine, cloth diapers were the gateway to a different level of political and cultural engagement on environmental issues.

Other Environmental, Economic And Health Impacts Of Diapering

In addition to their potential carbon footprint benefits, there are other reasons that parents choose to use cloth diapers over disposable. Disposable diapers are more expensive. The finance website mint.com estimated that even if you buy new cloth diapers and factor in the laundering, you will still save 27 percent in the first year ($584 for buying new cloth diapers and laundering vs. $800 for disposable diapers). Since my husband and I only spent about $100 by borrowing diapers or buying used ones, and washing our own diapers, our savings were even more significant. Disposable diapers also end up in landfills. The poop inside disposable diapers also ends up in a landfill instead of a water treatment facility, as happens when cloth diapers are laundered. Disposable diapers also contain materials that have a seemingly supernatural ability to absorb and retain liquid, thanks to a material called sodium polyacrylate (SAP). There is no evidence that SAP in diapers is bad for babies. Even brands that sell themselves as environmentally friendly like Seventh Generation use SAP, and claim that the absorbent gel is inert. Nonetheless, the use of SAP still leaves some parents feeling uncomfortable. As a result, some disposable diapers, like Tushies, have emerged that are both chlorine (as Seventh Generation is) and SAP-free.

Zero Footprint Options

The best option in diapering is to practice elimination communication from day one, and get your baby out of diapers as soon as possible. In our experience, that was easier said than done, however. Elimination communication halved our diaper needs, but we still needed diapers. If you are like us and cannot manage elimination communication all the time, you will have to make a choice between cloth and disposable. There is very little difference in the carbon footprint of cloth and disposable diapers if you cannot launder at home and line dry. The way that you use a cloth diaper will determine whether it has a lower carbon footprint than a disposable diaper. If you have to use a diaper service or a clothes' dryer, the energy used on the clothes dryer and/or in transit bumps the carbon footprint of cloth diapering just above that of using disposable diapers. Under other circumstances, however, the carbon footprint of cloth diapering can be nearly eliminated. With the purchase of used diapers, line drying, and installation of renewable energy, cloth diapering can have a very low carbon footprint, as low as 0.007 tons per year.

The financial cost associated with diapers is much more significant than the carbon footprint costs. Relative to housing, feeding, and other decisions, diapering is not a huge part of most families' carbon footprint, even with disposable diapers. Since cloth diapering is so much cheaper and can be a gateway drug to more environmental behaviors, I encourage everyone to consider cloth diapering. It is not a crucial decision when it comes to your carbon footprint, though. Using as few diapers as possible should be the goal for families that have already tackled more important actions to reduce their carbon footprint.

5.Feeding The Beast (Baby)

"A baby nursing at a mother's breast... is an undeniable affirmation of our rootedness in nature."—David Suzuki

"Eat food, not too much, mostly plants."—Michael Pollan

Even though babies eat very little, the way we choose to feed them can have an outsized impact on our carbon footprints. For the first year of their lives, babies cannot digest cow's milk, so they must either be given breast milk, or a formula that is designed to replicate breast milk. While it may seem obvious, it is worth confirming that breast milk is the better of the two options. And yet, despite a recent renaissance in breastfeeding, there is little support available to help breastfeeding moms understand what to do when their supply of milk seems too low or high, when nursing their baby is painful, or when other problems arise. As a result of this knowledge barrier, the Center for Disease Control's 2011 "Breastfeeding Report Card" indicated that 55 percent of babies in the United States were not being breastfed at six months of age, and only 15 percent were being exclusively breastfed. At twelve months, 76 percent of babies in the US were not receiving any breast milk at all.[1] This means that most babies in this country consume at least some processed infant formula.

Between the age of four to six months, babies begin to eat solid foods. Dehydrated and fortified rice cereal is a common starting food, as are sweet potatoes, bananas, avocados, and apple sauce. Later in the first year, yogurt, dry cereal, and a variety of vegetables, dairy products, and meats can be introduced. Conscientious parents may already be making efforts to eat locally, organically, and lower on the food chain, but in terms of the carbon footprint of foods, what are the best choices for our babies? Making baby food at home usually means using electricity for steaming and blending, which may entail the purchase of new appliances. The other main option, buying packaged baby food, requires transport of the jars or tubes the food comes in, and with it an assessment of the "food miles" the food has traveled. An alternative option is "baby-led weaning," where babies are mostly given the same food their parents eat.

In this chapter, we will talk about what to feed your baby at different points during the first year of their life, and the carbon footprint of each choice.

Breastfeeding vs. Formula

Intuitively, it would seem clear that breastfeeding is a better option for the environment than formula. Nursing a baby does not require any special gadgets that have to be purchased, and at first blush it does not seem to require any electricity at all. Of course, nothing in life is completely free, and in order to produce milk, most mothers need to consume extra calories, which equates to the consumption of more food.

Experts tell us that breastfeeding mothers consume an extra 500 calories per day, on average. This number is based on the calories in their breast milk. Since breast milk is about 20 calories per ounce, and babies eat about 25 ounces per day, the assumption is that most lactating mothers consume a little more than 500 extra calories in food.[2] Of course, this is just a generalization, as most mothers tend to eat whenever they have a spare moment, so the number of calories consumed can vary widely. In addition, the number of calories in breast milk differs between mothers, and with the age of the baby, which means that the calories consumed by each mother will vary. The carbon footprint of food per calorie also fluctuates widely. All of this means that the diet of the mother has a large influence on the carbon footprint of breastfeeding.

There is also some argument as to whether breastfeeding mothers need extra calories at all, as there is evidence that lactating mothers lose weight more quickly in the first months postpartum.[3] This suggests that, for the first three or four months, many mothers can produce around 500 calories of milk without consuming 500 extra calories worth of food. The reason for this is that these lactating mothers are burning stores of undesired fat accumulated during pregnancy in order to produce food for their babies—a very environmentally sound system! One could argue that the carbon footprint of turning body fat into food is actually negative, since you don't have to buy food and are creating something of value from something your body no longer needs.

Of course, after the period of maternal weight loss, most moms still consume the extra calories in order to maintain their weight. If a mother is consuming something low on the food chain, like lentils or other vegetables, the carbon footprint is around 1 kg CO_2e per kg.[4] The extra carbon footprint of lactation for these mothers is 3 kg CO_2e (6.6 pounds) over 8 months (assuming an extra 500 calories per day of a food low on the food chain). If, on the other hand, a mother is consuming something high on the food chain like lamb, the carbon footprint is around 39 kg CO_2e per kg, which means an extra carbon footprint of 2500 kg CO_2e (5512 pounds) over 8 months. Put simply, if a new mom eats something low on the food chain, the carbon footprint of her breastfeeding is negligible, whereas if she eats something high on the chain, it is mammoth—about 2.5 tons of pollution.

On top of the carbon footprint of additional food, most breastfeeding mothers in the US also use an electric breast pump either to enhance their milk supply or to allow others to feed the baby while they return to work or pursue other activities away from their child. The pump requires some electricity, as does the associated sterilization of bottles and parts. If the breast pump is only plugged in during use, and is used for an hour or less per day, the electricity consumption is quite minimal, around 0.1 kWh/day, or less than 5 pounds of carbon over 12 months.* If sterilization is only done for the first 4 months and in the microwave, that will require about 3 minutes per day of microwave use, or 5.5 kWh total and 7 pounds of carbon. If the breast pump and bottles are purchased new, the carbon footprint of manufacturing should also be considered. However, hospital-grade breast pumps that are made for multiple users can be rented from hospitals or breastfeeding centers. Also, many mothers (including me) ignore the manufacturers' warnings and use breast pumps that are borrowed from friends, eliminating the need for extra manufacturing.

Steps To Reducing Your Breastfeeding Carbon Footprint

- Eat a low-carbon footprint diet during pregnancy and lactation made up of foods that are low on the food chain and which are cooked in a less energy intensive way.

- Avoid disposable breast pads and breastfeeding gadgets. Try re-usable pads, or if you are not going out, consider a simple wash cloth or cloth diaper inside of a loose fitting sports bra. Many moms like special breastfeeding pillows. When I was nursing, I found a used feeding pillow, which I sold when I was done with it.

- Find used pumps and bottles, and use them sparingly.

- Use a manual pump, or even hand express without any gadgets. Confession: Given the difficulty of doing this, I end-

---

*In each case where I calculate the carbon footprint of using electricity I am assuming the U.S. average generation mix. If you have switched your home to renewable energy there will be no associated carbon footprint.

ed up using an electric pump. I tried, but could not extract enough milk manually at first, and the time investment of using the manual pump was not worth the relatively modest energy savings. I was always careful to unplug the electric pump when I wasn't using it, though.

Debbie And Ben's Feeding Story

Like many babies in America, Debbie and Ben's daughter suffered from allergies, which seemed to hit her particularly hard after she was nursed. After months of trying to identify and eliminate all of the potential allergens from Debbie's diet, her daughter was still in pain after breastfeeding, which pointed to her being allergic to something in the breast milk. At that point, Debbie and Ben's pediatrician recommended a vegetable-based hypoallergenic formula. It was very expensive, but it seemed to do the trick, as the baby finally seemed to stop having adverse reactions after breastfeeding.

Since Debbie and Ben could not choose the type of formula they were using, at first it seemed as if they would not be able to do much to lower their carbon footprint. However, they realized they could save both time and carbon pollution by having powdered formula delivered to their home in large batches, rather than driving to pick it up themselves. It was not the ideal option, but it was the best they could do for their carbon footprint at the start of their baby's life.

The Carbon Footprint Of Formula

The other option for newborns is infant formula. The first producer of formula, Justus Van Liebig, made it from a combination of cow's milk, wheat four, malted flour, and potassium bicarbonate, only to find later on that many babies failed to thrive on that concoction.[5] Although babies can do fine on formula today (as long as their parents have access to clean water and can afford formula after the free samples run out), both from a health and a carbon footprint perspective, infant formula is less than ideal. (In his book, *In Defense of Food*, Michael Pollan refers to formula as the perfect example of the hubris of believing that scientists can properly imitate natural foods.)

Nonetheless, for many families, infant formula is a necessary evil, so it is worth understanding its carbon footprint. Contemporary infant formula comes in either powdered form, as a liquid concentrate, or in a ready to drink liquid form. The powdered formula is either a mix of dried ingredients that have not been pasteurized after mixing, or a liquid formula that has been dried by spraying and high temperatures. A portion of the carbon footprint of formula comes from the production of its raw ingredients (e.g. feeding and raising cows), processing (mixing and sterilizing ingredients), packaging of the product (paper and tin), and the transport required to get it to your home (a drive to the store). It is in the manufacturing process of formula where calculating a precise carbon footprint can get tricky. Breast milk is composed of a combination of proteins, fats, and sugars that are dissolved in uncontaminated water, and the production of formula attempts to recreate that process. However, determining the carbon footprint of formula is not an exact science because formula contains many ingredients that have never been analyzed for their carbon footprint. Generally, the main ingredients in formula tend to be cow's milk or soy milk, which are mixed together with the other ingredients, pasteurized and standardized, before being packaged and sterilized.[6]

To get a sense of the carbon footprint of formula, we need to look at the footprint of its core ingredients. The carbon footprint of cow's milk varies depending on where the milk is produced and how the cows are raised. The factors involved include the land needed to raise the cows, the enteric fermentation (cow farts are powerful), plus transport and processing. Soy-based formula is often used for babies who have a dairy allergy. The Environmental Working Group's "Meat Eater's Guide" estimates an average of 1.9 kg CO2e per kg of milk and 2 kg CO2e per kg of soy product, so the carbon footprint of milk and soy is almost the same.[7] The amount of formula a baby consumes is related to their weight. A general rule of thumb is that you can multiply your baby's weight by 2.5 ounces to obtain their daily consumption amount. So, assuming that a baby consumes an average of 25 ounces per day for the first year (less at the beginning and end of the year and more in the middle), this comes to around 1100 pounds of CO2e for the first year of a baby's life.

In addition to the carbon footprint of the main raw ingredients, infant formula has significant processing and packaging costs. A conservative estimate for the yearly packaging carbon footprint of formula would be around 200 grams per week, for 52 weeks, or 10,400 grams of carbon, or 23 pounds, per year.[8] Transport can also be a major factor, especially if you live some distance from manufacturing sites and/or are driving long distances to procure formula.

Reducing Your Infant Formula Carbon Footprint

While breastfeeding has a lower carbon footprint than infant formula, there are still ways of lowering the carbon footprint of infant formula.

1. Don't drive to get the formula.

2. Use powdered formula. Ideally, you want a dry mixed formula to avoid the carbon intensive spraying and drying of liquid ingredients, but, as a consumer, the mixing process is not simple to determine by looking at the label on the product. Processing notwithstanding, powdered formula is less energy intensive to transport. It is also healthier for your baby, since liquid formula absorbs more chemicals from packaging.

3. Buy in bulk to reduce packaging costs.

4. Recycle all packaging.

5. Buy brands with less secondary packaging (shrink film, cardboard case, etc.).

After The First Six Months: Making Your Own Baby Food

Once you're baby reaches the age of six months of so, you can start introducing solid foods to his or her diet. Making your own baby food is a lower footprint option than buying food that comes in jars or plastic containers. "Making" your own baby food can be as simple as mashing a banana or an avocado with a fork. Even if you decide to use an appliance to steam and blend food, there is still relatively little electricity required to prepare your little one's food from scratch. In order to avoid the carbon bill of a new appliance, buy a used one, borrow one, or use appliances you already own.

Of course, the advantage of making your own food can be increased if you use lower energy forms of cooking. The microwave is one of the most efficient means of cooking food, and uses less than half the energy of an oven. In the summertime, the oven is even more of an energy hog because it loses so much heat, which either makes your house hotter or requires your air conditioning to work harder. Community ovens actually still exist in countries like Morocco, where I was a Peace Corps volunteer, so that families in the same neighborhood can share resources and avoid heating their homes in the hot weather.

Traditional baby food is usually made from fruits and vegetables that are pureed and then cooked. Simply mashing bananas and/or avocados with breast milk can provide a surprising number of meals. Sweet potatoes can be microwaved and mashed. Many other fruits and vegetables need to be cooked with some water or oil in order to soften them. To lower your carbon footprint, steaming vegetables is best done in the microwave, or in a pressure cooker on an efficient cook top, like an induction burner or natural gas powered stove top. Many vegetables, like corn, carrots, green beans, and zucchini can passively cook quite quickly if they are chopped into small pieces and submerged in a small amount of boiling water. For maximum efficiency, the water should be boiled in an electric kettle and reused for other dishes, or to passively heat surfaces in the home such as the baby's crib or bath towel. Just place any excess hot water in a pot and place the pot on your baby's bath towel or crib mattress. Pureeing baby food can be done in a food mill to avoid the use of electricity for blending. Small baby food purée kits often double as a bowl for feeding, and come with an ice cube tray for freezing extra food.

Growing Your Own Baby Food

Growing your own food, or getting food from a CSA, can have a lower carbon footprint than purchasing food from the store if you live in a climate where gardening is possible without the need for too much additional water or fertilizer. The key to having a low carbon footprint for home grown food is to use compost instead of fertilizer, and collected rain water, or grey water from baths or the sink. It is also important not to use extra energy to garden. A greenhouse that needs to be heated is a big drain on your carbon footprint.

Baby-Led Weaning

You can attempt to avoid the whole baby food stage by a practice known as baby-led weaning, or BLW, in which babies are offered regular food from the table to supplement what they get from breast milk or formula. This method allows babies to control their solid food intake by "self-feeding" what their fine motor skills allow them to pick up and chew. (Babies usually continue to nurse at regular intervals during the BLW process to ensure that they are getting the nutrients needed for growth.) The advantage of baby-led weaning is that parents will save energy by not having to prepare separate dishes for their children. This generally means that less food is wasted, since parents offer their own food to the baby, which they will usually eat themselves if the baby does not. For example, if the mother is eating a pasta salad with green beans, she might let her baby hold onto one long green bean stem and gnaw on it. Babies can also be given large items, like half an apple, or a bagel, to chew on. Steamed carrots (not pureed or strained, just in sticks) or cucumber sticks are also popular sides that everyone in the family can enjoy. I have also seen babies given an entire head of broccoli that is later washed and prepared for a meal. The key is to be alert and attentive when the baby is eating. Practitioners of baby-led weaning believe that if the item is too small for the baby to pick up by themselves, they are probably not ready to eat it. Cheerios are a great example of a food that is sometimes given to babies before they have the dexterity to use their thumb and forefinger in a "pincer grip" and pick up the cereal themselves. The baby-led weaning philosophy would avoid cereal until the baby can feed themselves with their fingers, and avoid purees until the baby can use a spoon or drink from a cup.

Without engaging in baby-led weaning, it is difficult to avoid wasting baby food, since babies often reject some or all of the food prepared for them (and, as most parents can vividly attest to, spoon-fed babies have a low ratio of food swallowed to food smeared on their cheek, into their ears, and even on their foreheads.) Sometimes I think that more baby food is washed down the drain than gets into the mouth of most children. Baby-led weaning isn't always cleaner, but it does eliminate some of the food wastage that goes along with trying to feed a small baby.

Edith And Frank's Feeding Story

Since their son Ian was at the bottom of the weight chart, many people in Edith and Frank's life encouraged them to feed him formula or fortified rice cereal in order to increase his weight. However, Frank and Edith could tell that Ian was doing well developmentally, despite the low weight. From day one, he had been an active baby, and seemed to burn the calories that he consumed faster than other babies. Not only did Edith and Frank not give in to the pressure to supplement Ian's diet with processed foods, but they also decided to engage in baby-led weaning, which meant a slightly lower intake of solid food at the start of the process.

When they ate their meals, Edith and Frank would simply let Ian grab pieces of whatever food he could hold on his own, with the theory that if he could pick it up himself, he was more likely to be developmentally ready to eat it himself. At first, he just sucked on green beans, but by eight months of age, he was feeding himself pieces of bread and lots of vegetables and fruits.

Environmentally Friendly And Baby Friendly Foods For Every Day Of The Week

For parents who engage in either baby-led weaning or make baby food themselves, one thing that can be very helpful is setting up an "eating template" for the week. For example, in our family, we eat a potato dish on Monday, a bean dish on Tuesday, pasta on Wednesday, eggs or tofu on Thursday, and pizza on Fridays. (On weekends, we free style.) I find that drawing up an eating template saves me hours of thought about what I'm going to make for dinner, and allows enough flexibility so that we're not always eating the same things. All our options are vegetarian, since eating low on the food chain is good for your carbon footprint, and all avoid using the oven, since it's the biggest energy user in the kitchen, other than an old refrigerator.

Keya's Low Carbon Eating Template

Potato Mondays

On Mondays, we eat potato curry, loaded baked potatoes, mashed potatoes with veggies on the side, sweet potato fries, or a potato salad. Here's one of my favorite recipes, for a loaded potato salad:

For six potatoes, poke three or four fork holes per potato and microwave (to save time and energy) for ten minutes. Slice the potatoes and put them into a salad bowl, and add the juice of one lemon, olive oil (I just pour what is probably about a quarter cup), salt (to taste), diced olives, sliced red peppers, and, if you have it, tons of mint. Sometimes I crumble a bit of soft tofu into the potatoes, and then mix it all up with a large serving spoon. To save even more energy, I sometimes use a crock pot for the potatoes. To do that, just poke a few fork holes and put the potatoes in the crock pot for two hours. (The crock pot uses about the same amount of energy as one of those old incandescent light bulbs, and barely heats up the kitchen—unlike those old light bulbs!)

Bean Tuesdays

On Tuesdays we eat a bean salad, refried beans, baked beans, daal, or a bean soup. Here's a good recipe for bean soup (I either prep this meal the night before and let it cook overnight, or else in the morning and let it cook during the day):

Slice up a few carrots (or whatever veggies you have) and garlic, add a splash of olive oil, and cover with water (about an inch for lentils and split peas and three inches for dried beans). Add a spoonful of vegetable bouillon, then cook it all in the crock pot on low for eight hours. If I have it on hand, I add a spoon or two of tomato paste.

Pasta Wednesdays

Pasta dishes can include a range of vegetables, macaroni and cheese with winter squash or sweet potato, and different pasta shapes and sizes. I boil water in my electric kettle, pour the boiling water over the pasta into a bowl, and then microwave everything for nine minutes. For the sauce, I use an induction stove. (We don't have natural gas in our house, so the alternative is conventional electric burners, which waste a lot of energy. Induction stoves heat the pot, rather than the air in the kitchen, and are the most efficient option.) Add a bit of olive oil to cover the bottom of the pot. Once the oil is hot, add a diced onion and 2 to 4 cloves of garlic. I then add 4 or 5 diced tomatoes, and cook for about 10 minutes, or however long it takes me to drain the pasta from the microwave. Throw in a few pinches of salt. In the summer, I add lots of fresh basil and oregano from the community garden in our neighborhood. (I can only keep mint alive in our garden, so am very grateful to the community gardeners who have offered to share their herbs.) In the winter, I use dried basil and oregano from the pantry. After I strain the pasta, I add it to the sauce on the stove and toss it all together. I usually serve with some shredded mozzarella on top.

Egg/Tofu Thursdays

I didn't introduce egg whites until my son was a year old, so before that Thursdays were simply "Tofu Thursdays." The menu includes baked tofu, tofu or egg curry, scrambled eggs, scrambled tofu, quiche, omelets, or sunny side up eggs. To make baked tofu, I prepare it the night before or in the morning by draining the water from the tofu, wrapping it in a wash cloth, cheese cloth, or cloth diaper that has never been used (this is also the best use I've found for those barely-absorbent Gerber cloth diapers). I place a weight on top of the wrapped tofu, such as a hardcover book. After anywhere between 30 minutes and 2 hours (depending on what else I'm doing), I unwrap the tofu and marinate it in a container of soy sauce, balsamic vinegar, olive oil, and herbs. I then broil it in the toaster oven for about twenty minutes with other chopped up vegetables on the side that I cover in any remaining marinade. The toaster oven uses less electricity than the oven, but still a fair amount, so when I make this during the day, I try to use our sun oven, which uses no electricity at all.

Pizza Fridays

On Fridays, I cheat. If I'm "making" pizza at home, I often just put some tomato sauce, mozzarella cheese and vegetables on toast and place it in the toaster oven. More often than not, we eat frozen pizza. To keep our cooking carbon footprint down, I take the pizza out of the freezer in the morning and let it thaw on the counter. I only buy pizzas that fit into our toaster oven so that I never have to use the oven.

Wasted Baby Food

A 2011 study by The World Wildlife Fund (WWF) in the UK showed that 3 percent of that country's greenhouse gas emissions came from wasted food.[9] In the United States, on the other hand, food represents the largest component of waste that ends up in land-fills every year, a total of 34 million tons annually.[10] In short, we waste nearly half our food in this country.[11] We spend energy, time and money growing, transporting, and cooking our food, and then just throw it away. Once in our landfills, this wasted food gets buried under so much other food so that it lacks exposure to oxygen, and in those conditions, the food breaks down and releases methane, a greenhouse gas that is twenty times more potent than carbon dioxide.

There are a few key things parents can do to waste less baby food and thereby keep it out of landfills:

1. **Labeling**. Write the date on breast milk bottles in the freezer and homemade baby food, and start doing it for all food. The act of labeling your food will hopefully remind you to eat it before it goes bad.

2. **Only put on his or her plate what your baby will definite-ly eat.** (And do the same for yourself.) Make sure you eat everything you buy. Baby food goes bad when there is saliva in

it, so just put a little food on your babies' plate at a time. Keep a clean spoon in the baby food jar or other vessel to transfer food onto the plate. Serve yourself smaller portions, too.

3. **Eat leftovers**. Most people save their leftovers, but sometimes forget to eat them before they go bad. Dating containers will help with this.

4. **Compost**. In the Peace Corps, we had a saying that it's "better to throw it out than to throw it up." Sometimes food really does need to be thrown out, but most of that food can be composted. Our compost is just a little ditch in our back patio area. It's nothing fancy, but it keeps our food scraps out of the landfill. Composting can be done indoors in a container, just remember not to add any meat or dairy to your compost.

Ten things to avoid if you want to lower the carbon footprint of your baby's food

Wasting food

Meat and cheese

Flown-in foods

Out of season foods

Packaging

Broiling things that taste just as good microwaved

Driving to obtain food

Buying baby food gadgets

Processed foods

Turning on the oven in the summertime

Our Feeding Footprint Story

Before my son Siddarth was born, it hadn't really been that hard to live without a refrigerator. My husband and I belonged to a CSA with a local farm that delivered food to us on a weekly basis. The leafy greens needed to be eaten in the first couple days, refrigerator or not, while the other vegetables and the eggs could easily survive out on the counter for a week, even during a hot Washington DC summer. (During particularly hot weeks, we would keep some vegetables in the basement, or eat them earlier in the week.) Unlike vegetables, eggs actually last even longer than a week outside of the fridge, and in many countries are not refrigerated at all. We really did need to eat everything we received within seven days, since the following week a new bag of vegetables and eggs would arrive. Overall, we wasted much less food because we could see all of our food out on the counter, so we knew what we had to eat. We didn't cook enough for leftovers in the summer, but in the winter we could keep food in a cooler on our back patio. The hardest part of not having a fridge was emptying it out in order to get rid of it!

While I was loathe to increase my carbon footprint once Siddharth was born, I really didn't think that it was going to be possible to live without a refrigerator once we had a baby at home. I couldn't figure out how I could be a breastfeeding, working-outside-the-home mom unless I had a safe place to store my milk. Pat Shelly, a lactation consultant at DC's Breastfeeding Center, told me that a conservative estimate for breast milk storage was the "rule of fives": it lasts 5 hours without refrigeration, 5 days in a refrigerator, and 5 months in the freezer. Once I learned that, I realized we would need both a fridge and a freezer.

We started doing research on the most efficient refrigerator options. This would be the only electrical item in our house that would always be turned on, so it had to be as efficient as possible. We considered getting a tiny refrigerator that would be cheaper and use less energy, but we had saved a lot of money by barely using electricity for the three previous years, and I wanted to use that money to invest in some of the cutting edge technologies of the future. We ended up getting a Sunfrost refrigerator, which was custom made for us since they do not receive enough orders for mass production. The fridge has thicker walls to keep the cold inside. The coils are located on top, so heat dissipates into the air, and not back towards the fridge, and it does not have an energy intensive auto-defrost feature so there is a pan of water under it that needs to be emptied monthly. It uses 105 kwh per year or 138 pounds of carbon, which is less pollution than a single car ride from Washington, DC to New York City. We also use it for baby food, which is hard to cook in single serve batches, and needs refrigeration.

We ended up using a mix of food in jars and homemade food when Siddharth was between 6 and 10 months old. Sweet potatoes cooked in the microwave, and mashed bananas and avocadoes, were some of his favorites that required little cooking energy. (We preferred to make our own, but could not manage our time well enough to always do that, and the energy savings from making our own food was not great enough to be compelling.) After Siddharth reached the age of ten months, we went with baby led weaning approaches, which essentially meant that he ate what we ate. This improved both the health and the carbon footprint of our diets—since we ate what we ate our baby ate, we had to employ extra caution. In the long run, we did end up with an increase in our carbon footprint, as we kept the refrigerator even after Siddharth stopped nursing. This meant we had to find some carbon footprint reductions elsewhere in our lives, such as reducing our carbon pollution from travelling in a car and by plane.

Zero Footprint Options

The zero footprint eating options are quite simple in the first year. For the first twelve months, breastfeeding combined with the mother eating a balanced diet that is low on the food chain (less meat and cheese) is the best option. The carbon footprint of breastfeeding depends on what foods the mother eats to meet the need for an extra 500 calories each day. If you chose lentils and vegetables, your footprint will be negligible. In the second half of the first year of your child's life, the nearly zero footprint option is to feed your baby what you are eating to avoid wasting food. This usually means making your own baby food or employing baby-led weaning techniques. Although your total footprint will not be zero, it will be zero for the first few months (if you use lose your pregnancy weight while breast feeding), and only slightly positive during the second six months.

6. The Child Care Dilemma

"America is 1 of 3 countries in the world—Papa New Guinea and Swaziland are the others—that does not have paid maternity leave."—Gloria Steinem

In many countries, a book about the first year of a baby's life wouldn't have to cover the topic of child care, as, outside of the United States, most parents are offered some form of paid leave for the birth of their child. In Germany, for example, new mothers receive 14 weeks of paid leave, while in France, 100 percent of the mother's salary is paid for 16 weeks. The United Kingdom offers 52 weeks of maternity leave with 90 percent pay, as well as two weeks of paid paternity leave. In Sweden, parental leave is for 420 days, and between the time available to mothers and fathers, can be extended for nearly two years. Simply put, child care for infants is not an issue for most new parents outside the US.[1]

Unfortunately, for parents in this country who work outside the home, decisions about child care have to be considered as early as the first few weeks of pregnancy. In some cities, child care facilities have waiting lists of longer than a year, and in most places in this country, it is common for babies as young as twelve weeks of age to spend forty hours a week or more in a child care facility, or with a nanny. Without paid maternity—or paternity—

leave as an option, decisions regarding whether or not to work outside the home, and if you do, deciding who will take care of your children, is a major decision facing most new parents.

Not having much, if any, leave means that most parents in this country need to have others take care of their babies. If you are aiming for a zero-carbon baby, this means tying to get other people to accept your worldview and your way of doing things. For some parents, this can be done successfully, while for others, compromise is required. This chapter will discuss the options for childcare that are available to most parents in this country, including child care facilities outside of the home, as well as a child care provider in the home.

Our Childcare Story

Two hours after I took my pregnancy test and told my husband we were having a baby, I found myself at work, sitting in my office, unable to concentrate. I went down to the lobby of the building, taking the stairs so that no one would see me. I then snuck over to a nearby child care facility and asked if I could put my name on their waitlist. The person at the facility took my deposit and told me to expect an opening in twelve to fourteen months. It felt odd telling this complete stranger that I was pregnant before I had told my family or friends, but I liked having the peace of mind of knowing I had gotten on a list at least one child care facility. At the time, however, it didn't occur to me to ask any questions about how the facility operated or what their policies were.

A year later, facing the end of my maternity leave, I decided to do a trial day in the infant room of the facility to see how it went. While I loved that the facility was energy efficient and in a LEED certified building, I didn't love anything else about it. In short, the place was a mess. They wouldn't use cloth diapers, so I had to go over and change my son's diaper myself every hour and a half. In addition, the facility was totally disorganized when it came to bottles, so much so that they fed my breast milk to another baby! They were also appalled at the idea of elimination communication and told me that it would do psychological damage if I took my baby to the potty before the age of three. The director also informed me that I could do psychological damage by not letting my baby eat the same food as the other children when I asked about vegetarian options. All in all, it was a terrible experience, and my husband and I decided not to send our son there, despite the convenience and the energy efficiency of the building.

Luckily, Andrew and I both had parents nearby who not only were willing to watch their grandson, but were also incredibly tolerant of our potty-going, breast milk feeding, anti-consumption, energy-saving ways. (They even got used to using public transportation to visit us: my mother-in-law made the two hour train to our house twice a week, while my father took a bus to the Metro three times a week.) As a result of their assistance, I was able to return to work for three days a week when Siddharth was four months old. When Siddharth was six months old, I started working full time. By that point, it was getting harder for our parents to continue to help us, so Andrew and I decided to try a child care facility near his office.

At the beginning, the routine was incredibly complicated. On Monday morning, Andrew would run into work with a jogging stroller, drop Siddharth off at the child care facility, and then lock the stroller up in the garage of his office. In the evening, he would take the Metro home, carrying Siddharth in a baby carrier. On Tuesday, he would take the Metro to work in the morning with the baby carrier, and use the jogging stroller to run home in the evening. Wednesdays were the same as Mondays, Thursdays the same as Tuesdays. On Friday, Andrew would take the Metro home, leaving the jogging stroller at work, and the following Monday he would have to take the Metro in to work—so he had to keep track of whether it was a Metro Monday or a running Monday at the start of each week.

It was a six-mile run each day, which both baby and father

seemed to enjoy, but the system was far too complex. Eventually, Andrew started using the Metro for the commute in both directions. After a month or so of this, we realized that our baby was spending more time than we wanted in transit, and Andrew wasn't getting his run in frequently enough, so we switched to using a part-time nanny share for three days a week when Siddharth was eleven months old. Our parents also returned to watching him one day a week each, which was the perfect amount of time for them to form a close bond without it being an unmanageable burden. The part-time nanny share was the ideal situation for us since it was across the street from our house and the nanny, like our parents, was happy to use our cloth diapers, give bottles on our schedule, and even take Siddharth to the potty on occasion.

The Carbon Footprint Of Child Care Outside the Home

According to the US Census Bureau, more parents use day care or a nursery than any other type of child care, other than care by relatives.[2] However, as my initial experience with one showed, not all child care facilities are created equal. If you aspire to have a zero carbon footprint baby for the first year, you will have to find a facility which is open to new ideas and willing to work with you on diapering, feeding, and toileting preferences. You also want a facility that is in an energy efficient building near your home or office in order to avoid increased emissions from transportation. However, you may not have access to a child care facility with open-minded teachers that is in a green building next to your work or home. In that situation, you will need to choose among the options you have and prioritize the factors that have the biggest effect on your carbon footprint.

Transportation To A Child Care Facility

Transportation is by far the most important factor in determining the carbon footprint of a child care facility. Even if you have to drive as little as two to three miles to a child care facility, those are miles that you would not have driven otherwise. Those two to three miles, twice a day, all year, in an average family car translates to nearly a ton of carbon pollution that will make your baby's life harder by contributing to climate change.[3] In addition to the added pollution, cars are more dangerous than the train or bus. By taking public transportation, you can engage with your baby while in transit, and even feed your child, rather than leaving him trapped in a car seat.

If you must drive, try to do as little as possible. From a carbon footprint perspective, it does not make sense to burn the gasoline to drive further to a facility that is willing to use cloth diapers because the carbon footprint savings from cloth diapers are small compared to that of driving a car. This does not have to be a trade off however; if you find a facility accessible by public transportation or walking distance from your office or home you can always work with them to help understand your environmental preferences.

Michele And Chris's Transportation Story

When Michele and Chris's son Luke was born, Michele was able to take a year of maternity leave, so they didn't have to worry about child care initially. Once Michele had to return to work, Luke was old enough to ride in a bike trailer. Every morning, Michele or Chris would put Luke in the trailer and take him to the family care facility a few miles away, where they would lock the trailer to a bike rack, drop off Luke, and continue their bike commute to work.

Michele continued to bike even when she was pregnant with her second child. Unfortunately, she was only able to take three months of maternity leave the second time, so her daughter Ariana was not ready for the bike trailer when the time came for her to spend time in the child care facility. (There was no bus stop near the child care facility.) As a result, Michele had to drive Ariana to the child care center. Eventually, Michele realized that she wouldn't need to use her car as much if she could convince the child care center to let her park there all day. They agreed to her request, and she then started her daily routine of packing both her babies and her bike in the car, leaving the car (and children) at the child care facility, then biking the rest of the way to work.

Energy Use In Your Child Care Facility

Since child care centers take care of so many children at once, the amount of energy per child is usually quite low. Also, when you utilize child care facilities outside of the home, your house will be empty during the day, allowing you to unplug heating, cooling, lights, and cooking appliances. Even assuming those energy savings at home, there are still many draughty, poorly insulated child care facilities that use more energy during the day than you could save at home even by switching everything off. In addition to poor insulation, some facilities may have inefficient appliances, such as old refrigerators. A tour can give you some insight into the energy efficiency of a facility, since you will be able to see if there are Energy Star refrigerators and insulated window treatments.

There is only so much you can determine by looking around, though. Ideally, you want to find a facility that a third party has found to be energy efficient. Buildings that are managed by people who are concerned about environmental issues sometimes have EPA ratings, or LEED certification from the Green Building Council. If your facility does not have any of those certifications, you may get them to consider such measures by asking questions and expressing interest. If you are really committed, you can also consider spending the extra time to talk to the facility about the energy savings of more efficient appliances and better insulation. You may even be able to engage other parents in a conversation about how to reduce energy costs at the facility. Consider starting a "green team" that helps the facility consider and implement energy savings.

Feeding

In the long run, your success at breastfeeding may hinge on how your child care provider feeds your baby. Are they willing to carefully time your baby's feedings in a way that will allow you to continue to breastfeed? Are they willing to put unfinished bottles of breast milk back in the refrigerator, or does the facility insist on throwing out any unused milk? In order to maintain the milk supply of the mother, ideally you want the baby to be hungry when he is reunited with mom, and to consume the same amount of milk that is pumped each day. Breastfeeding is all about supply and demand, and when there is demand for milk, the mother's body creates the supply. If you have a care provider who can only calm your baby by feeding her, you may not be able to maintain your milk supply. For example, if mom and baby are reunited at 5:30pm, but the baby had a bottle at 5pm, or has been fed more milk than allotted that day, the baby will nurse very little when mom comes home. That decreased feeding will in turn signal to the mother's body that she doesn't need to make as much milk the next day. Over time, if this trend continues, the mother's milk supply will continue to go down and breastfeeding will become impossible. Of course, some mothers have a more flexible milk supply that is not as responsive to daily changes in milk demand, while others have a more abundant milk supply overall, so this will not be as big a problem for all breastfeeding mothers.

Even when solids are introduced, feeding philosophies can still be an issue. Will your child care provider support you if you continue to provide breast milk throughout the latter part of first year of your child's life? Will they insist on feeding the baby solid food before you are ready to do so? Are they willing to maintain a vegetarian diet once solids are started? In many child care facilities, an external catering company provides food for the babies on solids. If this is the case, you may be able to circle the meals you are comfortable with your baby eating and cross out the meals for which you will provide food from home. There are also child care facilities that offer vegetarian menus for babies.

Cloth Diapers At A Child Care Facility

Another consideration for the carbon footprint of your baby is whether the facility is willing to use cloth diapers and cloth wipes or practice elimination communication. The main barrier to use of elimination communication in a child care facility is time, as the process requires that the provider pay attention to one baby over the others and spend time playing with them on the potty. This is generally not possible in most child care facilities. The chief obstacle to cloth diapering is not generally time, but rather cultural, and sometimes legal, issues. Many municipalities have strict rules for child care facilities concerning waste handling, and these rules make many facilities nervous about using cloth diapers of any variety. Over the long-term, parents can fight these rules by engaging local policy makers. A short-term solution that usually works is a note from a doctor saying that s/he recommends that your baby wear cloth diapers. It is also much easier to work with a facility where other low-carbon parents have already paved the way. If teachers have used cloth diapers before, they are usually amenable to using them again.

That said, very few child care facilities will be willing to use prefolds with covers, which are by far the cheapest cloth diapering option. Instead, most will require either pocket diapers, or all-in-one diapers. This is because each caregiver is usually responsible for up to three babies at a time, so they need a simple diaper that is as easy to use. Many facilities will also want to double bag the poopy diapers. This means that you will need cloth bags for double bagging, as well as a larger wet bag to hold all of the dirty diapers and cloth wipes.

Waste

Child care facilities can be incredibly wasteful places, particularly if disposable products are used on a daily basis. For example, many infant rooms of child care facilities use disposable booties that parents are required to wear before entering. One option is to find a facility that will allow you to remove your shoes instead of using disposable items. Or alternatively, explain that you are not comfortable with the disposable booties and that you would prefer to come in wearing clean socks.

Also, as is the case with cloth diapers, many facilities will double bag disposable diapers. However, some facilities have special diaper bins that trap the smell, which is preferable to all those plastic bags. In the case of food, many care providers will put jarred baby food into a Styrofoam bowl and feed it to the babies with a plastic spoon. In addition, many child care facilities do not practice recycling, and put glass jars and aluminum cans into the regular trash. Check to see if the facility you are considering recycles. You might be able to find a child care provider that uses reusable plates and cutlery or that allows you bring your own each day. If not, at least try and find a facility that lets you bring in a labeled spoon and bowl that you can take home every day. Who knows—your use of real cutlery could spread to other parents and actually change some practices! If nothing else, you will have paved the way for the next environmentally-minded parent who comes along. If the child care facility you are considering goes with a more wasteful approach, you may want to see if they would be open to other options before giving up on the facility altogether.

Ten Questions To Ask Your Child Care Facility

Is the facility accessible by public transportation?

Are they willing to put your baby on a potty periodically throughout the day?

Are they willing to use cloth diapers?

Do they double bag diapers in plastic bags?

Do they always warm bottles, and if so, how do they do it?

Do they have experience with the feeding schedule of a breastfeeding baby?

Are they willing to calm the baby down in other ways besides feeding towards the end of the day to ensure he is hungry for his evening feeding?

Do they use a dishwasher and reusable plates, or do they use disposable cutlery and plates?

Do they require the use of disposable hospital booties, or can parents take their shoes off?

Do they provide food, and if so, do they have vegetarian options?

Child Care In The Home

The primary alternative to a child care facility outside the home is having a grandparent or a nanny in your home, or in another parent's home. While having child care at home eliminates the need for you to travel an extra distance, often times it merely shifts the transportation costs to your provider, rather than eliminating the need for transportation altogether. Like with a child care facility, the carbon footprint of having a provider come to your home is also most affected by transportation. When interviewing nannies, you should find out whether they plan to drive to your home, and of so, how far they will be traveling. You may be able to find a child care provider who lives nearby by targeting listservs geared to your community, or by asking neighbors if they know anyone in the area. The further your provider has to travel, the higher your carbon footprint for child care. Some parents also consider a live-in or live-out au pair, which usually means that the provider has to fly in from another country. The carbon footprint of just one round trip flight between New York and Paris produces nearly a ton of carbon pollution, for example, and many au pairs naturally want to go home to visit at some point during their stay. That means that having a live-in au pair from another country is usually a bad option for a zero footprint baby.

One major advantage to having a child care provider come into your home is that you can hire someone who is more amendable to "quirky" parental requests like cloth diapers, elimination communication and breastfeeding than large child care facilities with formal rules and processes. If you are using cloth diapers, demonstrate to the provider how to do them during the interview process and ask if she or he is comfortable using them. People are usually more resistant to cloth diapers in concept than in practice, so showing how them it works, and changing a diaper in front of the prospective provider, is usually very helpful. Also explain any feeding and toileting preferences you have. Experienced nannies have many ways to calm a baby other than feeding, and therefore are usually comfortable following a feeding schedule. Elimination communications is still a relatively uncommon practice, however, and is the one thing that many providers are likely to resist. Again, showing your prospective nanny how you do it will help a lot. Also, be willing to explain to your provider the reasons behind the child care choices you have made. Realize too that you may have to compromise, and prioritize factors like transportation that will lower your carbon footprint the most over other practices.

Zero Footprint Options

Due to the absence of paid maternity and paternity leave, child care options for infants are quite scarce in many places in the United States. Finding any child care at all can be problematic if you do not have family members available to help. That means that you will probably not find a situation that is totally ideal. The reality is that if someone else is watching your baby they are not going to do everything the way that you would do it. Compromise and communication are key. Ask as many questions as you can up front so that there are no surprises. The most important factor to consider is transportation. Give preference to the options that minimize carbon pollution from transportation, since that is what will break your carbon budget. Child care providers who are within walking distance of your home are ideal, and child care that is accessible by public transportation is a very good second option. The best way to buck the automobile-centric high polluting lifestyle is to create a daily schedule that does not require a car. Remember that the benefits of avoiding driving for child care are enormous, and go well beyond reducing your carbon footprint. As your baby grows up, she will be safer in many ways, and healthier for having lived a lifestyle that included walking and using public transportation.

7. Family Size: How Much Is Too Much?

"Love the whole world as a mother loves her only child."—Buddha

"What do you think is the ideal number of children for a family to have?" That's a question that Gallup asks every few years, and not surprisingly, they have found that the answer to that questions tracks closely with fertility rates in the US. In other words, people tend to have whatever number of children they believe to be the ideal.[1] In 2011, just 4 percent believed that one was the ideal number of children to have, while a majority (53 percent) believed that two was the right number. Nearly a quarter of respondents (23 percent) said that three children was the ideal number, while eight percent believed that the perfect number of children was four—double the support for only children.[2]

Based on my personal experiences as the parent of an only child, I'm not surprised that so few people think having one child is the ideal number. From the moment I announced that I was pregnant with Siddharth, my friends and colleagues started asking me how many kids I planned to have. There seems to be a societal expectation that if you have had one child, you'll naturally want to have at least one more. And, questions about additional children don't just come from family and friends: for many moms and dads, watching their baby become a toddler stirs within them an overwhelming urge to have another baby.

But what about the carbon footprint of all these additional children? Is it possible to have a second zero footprint baby?

Is it right to have more than one child if you are a committed environmentalist? What is the relationship between population and carbon pollution? What is the impact of a baby in the first year? Beyond the first year? These are the questions I faced when deciding to even have one child, and many of the principles of thinking it through are the same no matter how many children you plan to have.

The Impact Of Adding A Person To The Planet

It may be heresy to say this, especially around new parents, but babies are just not good for the planet. Every time a child is born, the population of the Earth increases by one. The more people who live on the planet, the harder it is to provide sufficient food and water for everyone without doing permanent ecological damage. As a global community, we are currently using the natural resources of the Earth faster than they can be replaced—it currently takes the planet 1.5 years to produce the resources that we use in a single year. And if everyone lived like we do in the United States, it would take four planets to support our lifestyles.[3] Obviously we do not have four planets. As a result, we must learn how to live within the environmental constraints of our single world. That means fewer people, acting in more environmentally friendly ways.

Each individual on the planet does make a difference, particularly if they are living in a country that creates a lot of pollution per person. A fascinating 2009 study from Oregon State University calculated the carbon footprint of a baby in the US not only during the first year of its life, as we do here, but also through subsequent generations—making parents responsible for half of their kids, a quarter of their grandkids, etc.[4] Since the environmental future of our planet is impossible to predict, the researchers looked at three different scenarios: a pessimistic one, an optimistic one and one where things remained constant. In the most pessimistic scenario, greenhouse gas emissions continue to climb and future generations do not switch to renewable energy. In the most optimistic scenario, greenhouse gas emissions have been reduced thanks to policies that dramatically increase both energy efficiency and the widespread use of renewable energy. The final scenario was constant greenhouse emissions, or the status quo. The researchers then went on to compare the carbon footprint of having kids to the footprint savings from a number of modest lifestyle changes, such as buying a more efficient car, driving less, and insulating your home. The findings were astounding.

It turns out that in the scenario where there are constant greenhouse gas emissions, the carbon footprint of having a child in the US is 9,441 tons of carbon (including the carbon footprint of future generations). In the pessimistic scenario, the carbon footprint of a child is 12,730 tons. The carbon footprint of a child in either of those scenarios was enormous in comparison to the savings from simple measures like increasing the efficiency of your car (148 tons), driving a bit less (147 tons), and insulating your home (121 tons). In the optimistic scenario, however, the carbon footprint cost of having a child decreased to 562 tons. So, if parents got rid of their personal vehicle and opted for an electric car powered by solar panels, built a passively heated small house, and reduced their air travel dramatically, they could theoretically reduce their carbon pollution enough to offset the carbon cost of having one child, if and only if they also succeed in advancing policies like emissions trading systems, carbon taxes, or renewable energy tariffs that would reduce greenhouse gas emissions dramatically society-wide. Only in this scenario was it possible to have a zero footprint baby for its whole life—and even then, it was far from easy.

For me, the only scenario that matters is the optimistic one, which contributed to my decision to have a single child. The reason I consider the pessimistic and constant scenarios to be irrelevant is because the damage from climate change will be so great if either scenario comes true that it won't matter how many people live on the planet. For example, there is a small but real risk in the pessimistic scenario that global average temperatures could rise so high (increasing by 12 degrees Celsius or 21.5 degrees Fahrenheit) that "more than half of today's human population would be living in places where, at least once a year, there would be periods when death from heat stress would likely ensue after about six hours of exposure."[5] Deadly heat waves, strong storms, climate-dependent diseases and pestilence, drought, and wildfires all exist today, but in a world with even six degrees of warming, the severity and frequency of these events will increase so much that it will render many locations on the Earth inhabitable.

Thus, a world of constant or increasing greenhouse gas emissions to calculate the footprint of a child seems like an unpalatable view of the future. However, if you assume the optimistic scenario and work to ensure that society is successful in getting the right climate policies passed, then, with enough changes in your individual lifestyle, you could reduce your carbon footprint below what it would be without a child, even beyond the first year of your child's life. The bottom line is that you have to be both an optimist and committed to hard work in order to believe that you can have one child without increasing your carbon footprint . (Of course, you probably should be both an optimist and committed to hard work to have a child at all.) I believe it's better to be a parent of three, for example, who is truly committed to securing climate policies that will protect your kids' future than a child-free adult who does nothing to help transition the world to renewable energy.

What's The Right Number Of Kids For An Environmentalist?

People's preference for family size are affected by many factors, including the size of the family they grew up in, their experiences with siblings, social norms, economic costs, and views on what is best for their existing children. For most environmentally-inclined individuals, the prevailing idea that it's bad for the planet to keep adding people is also an important consideration. Taking all of this into account, there are generally three ways of looking at the effect of family size on the planet:

Attitude #1: "We'll only replace ourselves." There are two of us and if we replace ourselves, we're not causing any population growth.

Attitude #2: "We need to be kid free." The planet's atmosphere is a reservoir that is already quite full of pollution, and we should not take actions that add more pollution, like having children.

Attitude #3: "One and done." We know that adding to the population is bad for the planet, but we also need to slowly decrease the population, so having one child is a good compromise.

The first attitude lends itself to the conclusion that having two kids is the right number. If parents have kids at the "replacement rate," the argument goes, they are not contributing to population growth. Unfortunately, they are still adding a heck of a lot of pollution, especially if they live in the United States, where per capita emissions are around 20 tons, compared to the global average of 4 tons.[6] Keeping up with the "replacement rate" when it comes to having kids means adding greatly to the total stock of CO_2 in the atmosphere—a stock that is already above sustainable levels. There are currently almost 400 parts per million (ppm) of CO_2 in the atmosphere, and even at that amount, we are already experiencing severe climate impacts such as rapid Arctic sea ice loss and ocean acidification.[7] If you think of the atmosphere as a full bathtub that can hold 400 units of pollution and no more, then you can picture the challenge of reducing the amount of pollution in the bathtub. Not only do we need to stop adding to the bathtub, but we need to let some pollution go down the "drain," which in this case means letting it get absorbed by trees (which is quite a challenge when trees are also threatened by exacerbated droughts and wildfires caused by climate change.)

The second attitude, of having no children, leads one to believe that no additional pollution is tolerable. There is no question that, on its surface, this is the single best decision a person can make in terms of lowering their own carbon footprint. The argument that if everyone chose not to have children it would destroy the economy is not fundamentally sound because everyone is not choosing to not have kids. Remember the Gallup question about ideal family size? It turns out that only 1 percent of people in the US say that having no children is the ideal number. If people with green inclinations choose not to have children, they are doing something selfless, and giving the planet a gift.

Being adamant about zero population growth is not enough, though, as population is not the only environmental problem we are facing. In the United States, for example, population growth is already declining. In 2012, the Pew Research Center found that the average number of children that a woman is predicted to have in her lifetime is now 1.9, slightly less than the replacement rate.[8] Despite this decline, greenhouse gas emissions in this country are still enormous—a quarter of global carbon pollution comes from the US, and we only make-up 4 percent of the world's population. Our outsized carbon footprint is a result of using more resources than we need, and our unwillingness to transition to clean technology.[9]

The solution, then, lies in both reducing population and changing consumption patterns. We need to slowly decrease the population over time, while at the same time focus on switching to clean energy technologies. There are too many people today who do not have access to adequate food, water, and renewable energy, and with fewer people on the planet, it would be easier to address the poverty and climate crises. The Holy Grail is a world in which our washing machines, cars and ovens are powered by solar and wind energy, and there are also fewer mouths to feed.

We already have the technology we need to get to a renewable energy future—countries like Denmark and Germany are already doing it. In fact, in Germany, the economy has thrived during a massive transition to solar and wind energy. In the wake of the 2011 Fukushima nuclear disaster, there was a massive protest in Germany against nuclear energy.[10] Facing enormous public pressure, the government committed to shutting down their nuclear energy plants and switching to renewable energy.[11] The results were impressive. By 2012, a quarter of the country's electricity was being generated from renewable energy, putting Germany on track to meet their goal of 80 percent renewable energy by 2050.[12]

While not having children is definitely the best choice for the environment, it is not the choice that many environmentalists make, however. Paul Ehrlich, author of *The Population Bomb*, has one child, as does Bill McKibben, who has energized a generation of young climate activists, and Michael Mann, the climate scientist behind the famous "hockey stick" figure showing rapid global warming. As my husband and I were trying to decide whether to have a child or not, I could not help but look at the choices that those around me had made. One consideration for me was that a generation of people without kids might not have the same stake in the future as a generation of passionate parents committed to creating an environmentally sound would for their children. With this thought in mind, having one child seemed to be the most wildly optimistic action I could take, and it showed my commitment to ensuring a livable planet for the next generation.

Myths About Only Children

With two children being viewed as the ideal number by a majority of people in this country, there is a lot of pressure placed on parents of one child to have another. Perfect strangers have approached me on the train when I am with my son and asked when I'll be having another child, (and then proceeded to warn me that Siddharth will grow up to be selfish if he doesn't have a sibling). Even without factoring in societal pressures, the decision to not have a second child can be a difficult one. For some women, the desire to have a second child is nearly as great—or even greater—than the desire to have the first one, as something is activated in some women that makes them want to experience the baby period again. (Of course that urge is often suppressed after talking to a sleep deprived mother taking care of a newborn.)

For parents who have only one child, but feel the need for whatever reason to have more, it is worth reminding ourselves of the many benefits of only children. In *Maybe One: A Case for Smaller Families*, Bill McKibbren systematically busts many of the myths about only children, including:

Only children are spoiled and selfish. Twenty five years ago, researchers Toni Falbo and Denise Polit synthesized the results of 115 studies on only children and found that in terms of adjustment, character and sociability, only children are no different from other children. The only difference was that they were slightly smarter and slightly higher achievers.[13] It turns out that parents who spoil their kids have spoiled kids, regardless of whether they have one, two, or three children. There is nothing inherent about being an only child that makes a child selfish.

The economy would collapse if everyone had only one child. While it is true that with a lower birth rate there would be more older people and fewer younger people for a period of time, it's important to remember that people today are staying healthy longer and continuing to contribute to society well into their older years. In addition, there are economic and ecological consequences to overcrowding the planet. Since it already takes a year and a half for the planet to produce the resources we use in one year, having fewer people is likely to be more, not less, economically and ecologically sustainable.

Only children are lonely without siblings. It turns out that only children are just like other children. They are not any more lonely, and in fact may actually be spared the difficulties that some children with siblings face, such as severe sibling rivalry and reduced positive attention from parents. "Parents often view a second child as a gift for the first," writes McKibben, "but ironically it's precisely those olderborns who have the most playful, intense relationships with their mothers that treat their new siblings with the most hostility—and whose younger brothers and sisters are most hostile to them before they even reach their first birthday."

Michelle And Lee's Story

Michelle grew up in a family with two children, and assumed that she would have two children of her own as well. But after she and her husband, Lee, had their daughter, life got busy. In the first few years, Michelle was the primary caregiver, as Lee had to work a lot. While she loved being at home and spending time with her daughter, Michelle also found it hard to write, and do the work that she found most fulfilling. As a result, she was happy when her baby grew up and was no longer a helpless, crying, infant. Despite the ladies in the grocery store who told her she would pine for the early days, Michelle did not miss the sleepless nights or the feeding frustrations.

A few years later, a time came when Lee could be more flexible in his work, so he and Michelle began sharing parenting duties more equally. Now they could spend more time together as a family while still having time to pursue their own interests. The moment was just never right to have an infant in the house again. When people asked them about baby number two, their answer started out with "I don't' know, not yet" moved to "we might be done" and ended up with "we're done." Luckily, Michelle and Lee's friends and family were supportive of their choice, and never pressured them to have another baby. For the people who felt the need to share their anti-only child sentiments, Michelle pointed out that there are lots of only children that turned out well, including her husband Lee. The truth was, their family felt complete when the three of them were together.

In Defense Of Parents and Non-Parents

One thing that many parents often don't realize is that child-less couples constantly have to defend their decision not to have children. In her book *Why Have Children?: The Ethical Debate*, Christine Overall encourages people to stop asking non-parents why they are not having children. Instead, she suggests, parents should have to come up with a reason why they have chosen to have children. Somehow, it is socially acceptable to ask a couple without kids why they don't have any, while it's not acceptable to ask parents why they chose to have children.

Before my husband and I decided to have a baby, we had friends and family members imply that we would be selfish if we did not have a child. I see that kind of treatment of child-free colleagues and friends all around me, and every once in a while it spills into the media via pieces like "I Don't Have Kids. Deal With It," which was published in the *New York Times* in 2011. "Why, in a country so rich in diversity and differences, in a land where contrasts and distinctions are rejoiced and applauded, do child-free people still have to make excuses, why do we still stand out so much? It's almost the last remaining prejudice," the author of the piece, Karen Segboer, complained.[14] Her complaint is particularly valid because the act of not having a child may be the most selfless thing a person can do for the environmental health of the planet.

Parents of only children don't have it any easier. My husband and I constantly hear stories of how lonely our son will be when he grows up. Perfect strangers chide us not to spoil our child, and ask us when we are planning to have another baby. I don't take taxis very often, but on a pair of occasions when I took one with my son when he was a baby, I was asked by the driver if I was thinking of having another child. One of the drivers was an Ethiopian woman, who told me that if I did not have a second child, I would regret the choice for the rest of my life.

Jennifer and CJ's Story

A lesbian couple, Jennifer and CJ toyed with the idea of having a biological child but decided against it because neither of them particularly craved pregnancy, and their baby was not going to be theirs biologically anyway. Therefore, adoption seemed like a better option for them. They actually started the process on a whim. One morning, they were watching the local news and a little boy appeared in a feature on foster and adoptive care called "Wednesday's Child." He seemed like such a nice kid, so they called the number on the screen to see what they could do to help him. They hardly expected to get a call back, much less the nearly daily return calls urging them to become foster and/or adoptive parents.

CJ and Jennifer took the parenting classes that the city they lived in required, passed the home inspection with the requisite fire extinguisher in every room, and signed up for the required CPR class, which seemed a little silly since Jennifer was a doctor. But the CPR class never happened, as CJ and Jennifer ended up deciding to move before they took the class. Since they were now living in a new state, they had to start the adoption class process over again, which they did. Halfway through the process, they came to realize that, in their new community, they could have a lot of kids in their lives without having a child of their own. CJ's cousin lived nearby and her two children often stayed with CJ and Jennifer for days at a time. Friends in the neighborhood relied on CJ and Jennifer to help pick their kids up from school, and make them meals until they could get home. Their friends also visited regularly with their (our) children. Between all of that, CJ and Jennifer felt that their desire to interact with kids was more than being met.

Rather than thank them for all that they did for the many children in their community, CJ and Jennifer instead often felt the need to defend their decision not to have kids of their own to their friends and families. "You'll never experience the joy of pregnancy," CJ's mom lamented. "The reason that couples get together is to have kids" others told them. "You won't have anyone to take care of you when you get old" they heard over and over. "Why don't you want children?" It almost got to the point where they were considering adopting a child just so that people would stop asking them about it, but they realized that was not the right answer for them. Their story is not so different from those of many other childless couples, some of whom actually do get pressured into having children.

Zero Footprint Options

The best choice for the planet is to have as few babies as your heart will allow. Also, make it easier for others to choose not to have children by not asking them questions as to why they don't have kids. Let other adults without kids into your child's life. Having one child is not great for the planet, but the associated pollution can be overcome with a commitment to rejecting fossil fuel use. It isn't possible to reduce your emissions enough to eliminate the impact of two children if you include the total impact of that child over their children and grandchildren's lives. However, some parents of two or more children are the very members of society that have the most at stake, and therefore work the hardest to ensure that the future of the planet is safe for their children.

8. The Adoption Option

"Biology is the least of what makes someone a mother."—Oprah Winfrey

If you want to grow your family in the way that is least harmful to the environmental health of the planet, adopting a child from within this country is the best option. There are over 100,000 children in the United States who are in foster care and ready to be adopted in any given year.[1] By adopting one of those children, you are not adding to the population of the planet, and are giving a child in need a home. Of course, there are many children in need of a home in other countries as well, and many parents choose to adopt internationally. In this chapter, we will explore three topics related to adoption. First, we will look at the reasons that people give for adopting, or for not adopting, as the case may be. Second, we will look at the carbon footprint associated with different types of adoptions. Finally, we will discuss the special circumstances facing adoptive parents who aspire to raise a zero carbon footprint baby, such as bringing an older infant into your home, and not knowing how long your nesting period will last.

Why Don't More People Choose Adoption?

In 2007, the Dave Thomas Foundation for Adoption did a survey of the American public aimed at "dispelling myths and misperceptions about the foster care adoption process." The results of the survey exposed some interesting prejudices, as well as some hopeful attitudes. Generally, people think adoption is a great idea. According to the survey, 72 percent of Americans had a very favorable view of adoption, with over 30 percent saying they had considered adoption themselves.[2] Based on those numbers, if only 0.2 percent of Americans who thought about adopting a child from the foster care system actually did so, there would be no children in this country in need of a home. The problem is that, despite a high level of theoretical support for adoption, widespread misconceptions about the foster care system keep many from actually going through with the adoption process. Among the core misconceptions are that many of the children in the system are juvenile delinquents; that not many children are actually awaiting adoption; that a majority of the children awaiting adoption are African-American (only 32 percent are); and a belief that most kids "age out" of the system when they turn eighteen—only 21 percent do. One of the most common fears from over 80 percent of the respondents to the Thomas Foundation survey was that the birth parents would try to regain the child—something that statistics show very rarely happens. There were also numerous incorrect notions about the types of parents that can provide a healthy environment for adopted children, including biases against single, older, and same sex parents. Taken together, these misconceptions about adoption not only keep thousands of children from finding supportive homes, but also hold back a process which is the best for the environmental future of the planet.

Fighting The Urge To Not Have A (Biological) Child

As we explored in the previous chapter on family size, assuming the "optimistic" scenario for greenhouse gas emissions, the carbon footprint of a child will be 562 tons, including the pollution throughout their lives, and that of half of their children, a quarter of their grandchildren, and so on. That means by deciding not to bring an additional person onto the planet, parents who adopt rather than have a biological child are avoiding 562 tons of carbon pollution, which is similar to the reductions you would get by making all of the other changes in this book. Unfortunately, the decision to adopt for environmental reasons can be particularly difficult, since many people do not think that adopting a child is as good as having a biological child. If you adopt, you have to be comfortable with people assuming that you are infertile, for example.

In addition, you may have to fight against your own biological urge to have children of your own. To this day, I can barely explain to myself why I chose to have a biological child rather than adopt. It was an intangible urge that eludes logical explanation. I'm so grateful for that urge and for my Siddharth, who has brought me immeasurable joy. But I see that my friends who adopted also have immeasurable joy with their children. The fact that I wasn't able to fight the biological urge to procreate makes me all the more respectful of my friends who chose to adopt in the face of such a strong desire. I imagine that it's a little bit like being vegetarian—for some people, it is an easy thing to give up meat, and even if there is some biological urge to eat meat they are suppressing, it is not an overwhelming urge. That was the case for me when I became a vegetarian in college. It was not hard for me to give up meat, and I have never craved it since I quit the habit. However, I know other people who absolutely cannot (and would not want to) suppress the urge to eat meat, despite being avid environmentalists and knowing that vegetarianism causes less pollution. Similarly, it wasn't possible for my husband and I to suppress the urge to have a biological child, so we worked as hard as we could to reduce our carbon footprint in other ways. Mary and David are two friends of ours who resisted the biological urge to have children, and instead adopted a beautiful family.

Mary and David's Adoption Story

When Mary and David decided that they wanted to start a family, they did not even consider having a biological child, as they did not wish to add to the population of an already overpopulated world. Mary had grown up having some familiarity with adoption as her mother had been a social worker in the foster care system. That exposure made her understand at a young age that there were children out there who needed homes. It also left her familiar with the challenges typical of adoption through foster care. As a result, Mary didn't think she and David were ready to navigate that process on their first adoption. Private adoption also did not appeal to them because they wanted to give a home to a child who needed one the most. International adoption seemed to be the best fit for them.

Mary and David chose an agency and country (China) for adoption based on where there was a need for adoptive parents, and where the adoption process seemed to be the most transparent and ethical. It took four months to get their paperwork in order, and it was another seven months before they were matched with their daughter. While birth mothers count the weeks by their growing bellies, Mary and David were kept up to date by their agency, and through the community of other parents who had submitted dossiers during the same month. There was even a website where they could monitor their progress towards bringing home their baby. Since they only found out the age and gender of their child two months before bringing her home, Mary and David brought very little during the nesting period.

Finally, the big day arrived and Mary and David booked their flights to China. The moment they first laid eyes on their daughter, they knew that they had made the right decision. A few years later they adopted their second daughter from Vietnam. The urge to have a biological child was not a factor for them, as they knew they wanted to adopt and avoid the pollution of increasing the population of the planet.

Different Types of Adoptions

The vast majority (86 percent) of adoptions in the US are domestic, and about half of those are public agency adoptions of children in the foster care system. The remaining 14 percent of adoptions are international adoptions that bring children from other countries to the United States.[3] Not surprisingly, there is a big difference between the carbon footprint of international adoptions compared to domestic adoptions, so in the following sections they are each explored separately.

International Adoptions

While the percentage of international adoptions is small as a total percentage of adoptions, there are still nearly 18,000 international adoptions every year in this country. There have also been a number of high profile celebrities like Angelina Jolie and Brad Pitt who have chosen international adoption and given it a higher profile in the media. Given the high carbon footprint of international travel and the high carbon footprint of raising a child in the US, it is not immediately obvious whether the carbon footprint of having a biological child or adopting a child internationally would be greater. To figure this out, I calculated the carbon footprint of a hypothetical international adoption.

In the case of international adoption, a baby is being brought from one country to another, and usually this move is from a country with relatively little carbon pollution to a country with high amounts of carbon pollution, such as the United States. For the purposes of this book, we are looking at the entire family's carbon footprint for the first year of a baby's life. In that context, the carbon footprint of the adoption depends on how long the baby spends in her birth country, and when she moves to her new home, as well as the number of flights the adoptive family needs to take in the first year, and the number of people travelling on those flights. I'll use a hypothetical adoption from Vietnam by an average family in the United States to demonstrate this. Assuming two round trip flights for two adults, the carbon footprint of the flights is over 7 tons of CO_2.[4] Since per capita emissions in Vietnam are around 2 tons of CO_2e per person, and in the US they are around 20 tons for the first year, the longer the baby is in Vietnam, the lower her carbon footprint.[5] Assuming that the adoptive parents get to take their baby home at 10 months of age, that baby is increasing the family's carbon footprint by an average of only 6 tons in the first year. If the adoption did not take the place of a birth in the US, the carbon footprint includes the 7 tons from the flights and the 6 tons from bringing the baby to a high carbon footprint country, for a total of 13 tons. If, on the other hand, the adoption is taking the place of an additional US birth, than it is fair to note that 13 tons of carbon is less than the alternative of raising a baby for one year in the US. If you assume average emissions of 20 tons for a person in the US, the adoption still has a carbon benefit of 7 tons.

However, the only reason that the carbon footprint of the first year is so low is that the first ten months of the year are spent in Vietnam rather than in the US. In subsequent years, this hypothetical child will be increasing her footprint well above what it would have been in Vietnam. Parents should also factor in the carbon footprint of flights to the country of origin when the child is older, for cultural reasons. Throughout the course of your child's life, the carbon footprint of an international adoption is much higher than that of a local adoption because of the additional travel and because of the higher carbon footprint of a person in the US. By talking about that carbon footprint later in life, I do not mean to imply that international adoption is a bad idea or that adopted children should not visit their country of origin when they are older. In fact, there are many good moral arguments for international adoption. However, the goal of this section is to arm expectant parents with information about the carbon footprint associated with various options, and there is definitely a higher carbon footprint for international versus local adoption.

Local Adoption

Unlike international adoption, or even domestic adoptions over long distances, local adoption does not have associated carbon emissions from flights. Local adoptions also have the carbon footprint advantage of not transferring a baby from a low-polluting country to a high-polluting country. The reality, however, is that for some people, adopting locally presents a range of difficulties that are not associated with their carbon footprint. The birth mother may have more rights, for example, so the legal process and period of uncertainty may be longer. Also, as with international adoptions, many children are older and/or have special needs. Even if adoption rates went up for local adoptions in the US so that it was even more difficult to adopt an infant, special needs and older children would still need homes. There are few people willing to tackle that challenge, but my friend Brian is one of them.

Brian's Adoption Story

Brian was always an environmentalist, but the more he learned about the forecasted impacts of climate change, the more dedicated he became to not having biological children. He didn't want to add to the number of people requiring resources, and was concerned with the moral implications of procreating in a world that is currently not committed to seriously addressing climate change. He did, however, care about the next generation and wanted to play a role in raising a child.

As a result, he decided to become a mentor with DC Family Youth Initiative, which works with foster children in Washington, DC. He was paired with a teen in the system, and spends time each week with him, so that the child's foster parents get a break, and that no matter what home the child is in that month, Brian remains a steady presence in his life. At first, the program was an intellectual exercise for Brian, as he wanted to see if he could play a role in parenting without being a biological parent. But after spending a year with his foster child and his child's friends in the program, he became increasingly invested in their future welfare. He also learned more about the foster care system as a whole, and found out that there are currently more than half a million foster kids in the US in need of a home. Brian's passion for not having biological children turned into a passion for caring for foster children. He is a dedicated mentor to an amazing boy. However, single parenting is not something Brian is ready to take on. If and when Brian finds a woman who shares his values to co-parent with, he looks forward to not just bringing foster children into his life, but also into his home.

Two Keys To Lowering The Carbon Footprint Of Your Adoption

The basics of lowering your carbon footprint remain the same whether you are adopting your child or having a biological child. Your home and means of transportation remain key considerations.

1. Strive to make your home as low carbon as the birth place of your child, if you adopted internationally. However, whether or not you adopt a baby, we should all strive to lower our emissions to the global average, which is 4 tons, compared to an average of around 20 tons in the US. In the case of international adoption, another goal might be to reduce your carbon footprint to that of the birth country of your baby. For example, if you adopt a child from Vietnam, you might consider installing enough solar energy on your home to keep your carbon footprint as low as the per capita footprint in that country.

2. Minimize carbon-intensive modes of travel like flying in an airplane, or reduce the number or length of those trips.

Adoption Nesting and Consumption

Adoptive parents feel the same urge to nest as biological parents, and therefore most of the tips in the chapters on nesting and baby gear are equally applicable to adoptive parents as they are to birth parents. One challenge is that adoptive parents do not always know how much time they will have to prepare for their baby—the nesting period can be anywhere from four months to ten years.[6] No matter how long it takes, adoptive parents should still focus as early as possible on large projects like installing renewable energy and increasing insulation and efficiency so that these things will be in place when the baby arrives. If renewable energy installation is not an option, consider switching to green energy through your utility, and start eliminating appliances that use energy. By recycling appliances that you can live without, like electronic gadgets or a clothes dryer, you will save electricity and money throughout your baby's life. One of the biggest stresses of adoption is the uncertainty around when the baby will arrive, or if he or she will arrive at all. Although the wait is stressful, consider passing the time with projects that will leave a better planet for your baby whenever he or she comes—and even if, sadly, he or she doesn't.

Although waiting for your baby is hard, one advantage for adoptive parents is that they are blessed with a built-in excuse for avoiding much of the over-consumption associated with babies. *"I would love to have a baby shower, but I don't know when the baby is arriving, I don't know the gender of the baby, or even the age."* I am grateful for the thoughtfulness of everyone who has ever given us baby gifts, but I would have loved to have an excuse like that to avoid much of the consumption associated with giving birth. Of course, if you do decide to have a baby shower, you can also ask for used items and minimize the carbon footprint of the event itself.

Feeding Your Adopted Baby

Adoptive parents will need to re-think decisions about feeding once they find out the age of their child, as they may discover that they are not dealing with a baby at all, but a toddler or older child. (For international adoptions, it is unusual to bring home a newborn baby). If parents are pursuing a private adoption of a newborn, breastfeeding can be an option, though not all adoptive mothers are able to initiate lactation in response to their adopted baby. Even for mothers that can lactate, it is unlikely that milk production will be sufficient to meet the nutritional needs of the baby. [7] If an electric pump is used, there will be a small increase in the carbon footprint of breastfeeding for adoptive parents.

Because of the difficulty in breastfeeding adopted babies, most adoptive parents end up using formula. The best approach in this case is to limit the amount of driving you do to procure the formula and buy in bulk to minimize packaging, once you know what formula your baby prefers. One of the unique challenges of an adopted baby is that you may not be able to replicate the formula and nipple that your child is used to from his place of birth. In the case of international adoptions, you will need to bring some formula from your baby's birth country home with you and mix it slowly with the formula that you can buy in the US. Slowly increase the share of the domestic formula over time until your baby will take it exclusively. You will also need to have nipples for bottles that the new baby will take. Bring at least one bottle from your baby's birth country so that you have something he will drink from in an emergency, and try other bottle nipples after you arrive home. Consider asking three or four different friends with babies if you can borrow one of their bottle nipples, so that you have a variety on hand that you can try with your baby. You may also ask your pediatrician and friends if they have small samples of baby formula, so that you have a few different types on hand. Just like with a biological child, figuring out how to get your adopted baby to take a bottle or eat is a matter of trial and error.

In An Ideal World...

Many parents in the United States adopt babies from disadvantaged countries in order to give that child a better life, but ironically, providing a child with a better life in the US could also mean giving them a much larger carbon footprint. Since 1960, the human population of the Earth has doubled, reaching seven billion in 2011, but all of those seven billion people do not pollute in the same way or use resources at the same rate.[8] It matters quite a bit how those people behave, what resources and technology they use, and how they generate energy.

Imagine three different types of lifestyles: First, we have a baby born in Mali who grows up in a small home without electricity, with minimal consumption, and with nearby land where his family grows their food. To cook their food, the family uses branches from a nearby tree nursery in a small cook stove. The clothes that baby wears are passed between families. As the child grows older, he plays with leaves, rocks, and sticks instead of toys. On the other end of the spectrum, imagine a baby born in Texas, who grows up in a large home with central heating and air conditioning, which are powered by a coal-fired power plant. That child lives far from social centers and food, so petroleum is required for daily transportation in a car. Every month, new toys and clothes are purchased for this child, whose main leisure activity is watching a television, which also uses electricity from the coal-fired power plant.

Our third scenario is the middle of these two extremes, a baby from Germany who grows up in small home that is heated using electricity generated mainly from wind and solar energy. This child's home is connected by public transportation to schools, social centers and even food production centers. There is limited space for toys and clothing in the house, and as a result, consumption is low. Leisure activities are more likely to involve friends and family rather than anything with an electrical plug. Food is mostly imported from far away, but local, seasonal foods are also a part of the family diet. This baby has a carbon footprint somewhere in between that of the child in Mali and the one in Texas. When it comes to energy use, all countries should aim to be more like Germany, and Germany should aim to go even further in the direction of Mali by providing 100 percent renewable energy to their citizens and producing goods locally, so that their residents can stop producing greenhouse gas emissions altogether. In a world like that we would have less inequality, and less worry about where we adopt from.

Zero Footprint Option

Choosing adoption as a way to grow your family will lower your family's carbon footprint for generations to come. Adopting a child also results in one fewer person on the planet, assuming that the adoption takes the place of having a biological child. However, for international adoptions, the carbon cost of long flights can be significant, and the increased carbon footprint of a lifestyle in this country is quite large in comparison to most countries that babies are adopted from. Local adoptions, on the other hand, have almost no carbon footprint, assuming that you use public transportation to get to adoption classes. Unfortunately, there is an unknown waiting period for parents who want to adopt a child. While this waiting period can be torture, it can also be used as a time to lock in many low-carbon lifestyle changes that will lower your carbon footprint. Adoption can also be used as a great excuse for avoiding all of the consumption involved with new babies and encouraging friends and neighbors to shower your baby with their loving presence instead of new toys and clothes that will only be used for a few months.

9. Bringing Others On Board

"A dream you dream alone is only a dream. A dream you dream together is reality."—John Lennon

Despite some strides in awareness over the past few years, the cultural traditions around pregnancy and baby-rearing in America still revolve around profligate consumption. Think baby showers and children's birthday parties featuring piles of boxes filled with gifts, and the associated mountains of ribbon and wrapping paper. As a new parent interested in raising your baby in a sustainable fashion, it isn't easy to swim against the current of societal expectations, which dictate that people buy "things" for babies, and that parents be happy to receive those things.

It's even harder to stand up for your beliefs when you don't have a support system of like-minded friends or fellow parents, or when one parent or a grandparent is not fully on board with the concept of getting through the first year of your baby's life without increasing your carbon footprint. However, it is vital to engage your skeptical friends and family in a discussion about the lifestyle choices you want for your child. By explaining to them why you are doing what you are doing, you can use baby-rearing as a jumping off point to try and alter the societal norms that are destroying our planet. While at first you may be accused of being anti-social, or even ungrateful for asking friends and family to refrain, for example, from giving gifts to you and your baby, in the end, your individual actions can bring about a cultural change towards simplicity, and that is a gift everyone can cherish. A simple life means fewer manufactured toys in your home, and a greater engagement of the imagination on the part of you and your child to turn everyday objects into toys. A simple life also means fewer carbon-intensive long trips, and more exploration and enjoyment of nearby sights. A simple life means less consumption, and more sharing.

My Baby Shower Story

Although I didn't want a gift-giving event as part of my pregnancy, my friend Leah and my mother wanted to throw me a baby shower, so to make them happy, I agreed to one. I went into the experience thinking that it was going to be a consumption nightmare, but came out of it with an appreciation for the creativeness of my friends and family.

I had laid down the rule that I didn't want any new items and didn't want anyone flying in from out of town for just one day. However, when posed with the challenge of "what to do for Keya when she doesn't want anything," everyone stepped up to the plate in wonderful and humorous ways. One of my mother's friends emptied out her grandkids' closets, and washed, sorted, stacked, and bundled clothes and other items so that they together provided an entire wardrobe for the first year of my son's life. Another friend of my mother's gave me a blanket that had been well-loved by her grandson, wrapped in used grocery bags that were decorated with items from the elementary school classroom where she taught.

To add some needed levity to what probably seemed to most people as my out of the ordinary wishes, Leah came up with a hilarious pub quiz about what wacky eco-friendly things my husband Andrew and I would do as our baby grew older. One question asked, "What will Keya and Andrew give their son for his sixteenth birthday?" The possible answers were:

A) A new electric car with a renewable energy-powered plug

station

B) A new bike

C) A new pair of walking shoes and a map of the city

D) A "SmartTrip" card with a year of Metro and bus fare

Of course, not everyone clearly understood what I wanted. One member of my family only heard that I wanted "diapers" instead of the full message that I wanted "used cloth diapers." Luckily, we were able to return the diapers quite easily without an extra trip. We also returned other items, including toys and books. We already had quite a few used toys and books, and we assumed that the people giving the gift wanted to make us happy rather than overburden us with things we did not need or want.

Overall, what made the process of avoiding gifts easy for me was having supportive friends and family. It also helped that I had already set the tone that I didn't want stuff by engaging in what I called the "compact" for a few years, when I bought nothing new at all. The compact meant I agreed with a group of a few thousand others that we would challenge ourselves to buy only used clothing or 100 percent recycled items. We also bought local food products, but if my coffee grinder broke (which it did), I asked my friends if they had an extra one in their basement or searched yard sales until I found one used. Since many of my friends and family knew about the "compact" thanks to a story on the local news, no one was too surprised when I said I didn't want anything for my baby unless it was used or specifically aimed at helping us reduce our footprint. In addition, instead of registering for my baby shower at a store, I set up a spreadsheet as a Google doc and listed the used items that I wanted to receive. I asked people to check off the items that they could either lend me for a few months or buy at a consignment shop or on Craigslist.

While the baby showers went well, throughout the rest of the first year of our son's life, we found that some people didn't know that we were trying not to acquire things, so we did receive gifts of new items. When this happened, I attempted to graciously accept both my defeat and the gift, which was usually a lovely item that was purchased with the best of intentions. I must admit, though, when I could do it on public transportation, or without making an extra trip, I returned the items to the store, donated them to a family in need, or saved them for the baby shower of a person who liked new things.

Zero Footprint Baby Party Ideas

Baby showers, baby naming parties, and holidays are occasions during your pregnancy and baby-rearing when consumption by others is expected. As the holidays approach, for example, parenting message boards become littered with threads about how to ask grandparents to give fewer gifts. Even parents who are not attempting to raise a zero footprint baby in the first year tend to get overwhelmed by the amount of stuff given to their baby at a time when the baby is barely aware of the toys around them, and in fact likely prefers the paper or box the toy came in to the toy itself. There are very few babies we know who do not already have more than enough stuffed animals and board books. Whether you are throwing a baby shower, a baby naming party, a bris, or a holiday party, events for your baby do not have to magnify your carbon footprint or make your closets bulge. Here are some steps you can take:

1. **Just say no to new gifts**. Ask friends and family to buy used items, or 100 percent recycled items. If they must buy something new, ask that it be something that you would have had to buy new anyway (e.g. eco-friendly washing detergent).

2. **Ask for homemade cards on recycled paper.** As I have learned, people make the most amazing cards when you tell them what you want. An old magazine can suddenly be "upcycled" into a beautiful baby shower card by your creative

friends!

3. **Have the event near public transportation and/or bike routes.** You can't force people to get out of the car, but you can make it possible for them to do so.

4. **Send an e-invitation or use recycled paper.** Make the invitation process simple by sending it electronically or just calling and inviting your guests. If a paper invitation is necessary, then use 100 percent recycled cards.

5. **Ask for help.** In lieu of a gift, ask your friends or family for help with preparation or clean-up. Tell them that their time is more valuable to you than any gift.

Grandparents

There is a theory that postulates that humans live so much longer than we should for our size because of grandparents. Basically, there is evolutionary selection for longevity in humans because infants with grandparents had a greater chance at survival. Just like today's parents, early human parents had to go out and bring home the bacon, so to speak. If there were grandparents around, the babies were more likely to survive, so evolution selected for genes associated with longevity.

Based on this, it seems like grandparents are biologically wired to want to do everything they can to care for their grandchildren. If your baby is lucky enough to have multiple living grandparents in good health, it is important to remember that they can be a wealth of information on low-carbon baby raising techniques, as many of our parents lived in a time when it was normal to have glass milk bottles from a local farm, when items were repaired and not replaced, and when an airplane flight was uncommon, so they managed in a car or train with a baby.

However, you may find that your parents and in-laws do not share your ideas about zero carbon footprint baby-rearing. Some grandparents love to buy gifts, take flights or long drives to see their grandchildren at regular intervals, and give baby-rearing advice that may or may not be consistent with your philosophies. How can you gracefully ask your in-laws and parents to give fewer gifts? First, tell them that you would very much like them to respect your wishes and not give gifts. If they want a further reason, try talking about your concern about the amount of raw materials needed to produce the toys and clothes for the baby. If they don't care for the environmental argument, try telling them you don't have room for more items. If all else fails, simply tell them that they can buy items, but the toys and clothes they buy need to stay at their house for use during visits. Since most baby clothes can only be worn for a couple months, this should cut down on the purchase of new clothes. And the grandparents also probably only have so much room for new toys!

Coping With Family And Friends Who Are Not Supportive

Not all of our friends and family were completely supportive of the decisions that we made in an effort to eliminate any additional carbon footprint in the first year of our baby's life, or to engage in the political processes needed to bring about a renewable energy future. However, I learned a few things about how to cope with those who are not (yet) fully supportive:

1. **Stand up for yourself.** Be firm and clear about your preferences and what works for you and your baby (it turns out, this will prove useful in many matters, not just your baby's carbon footprint). Be clear about what kinds of gifts are acceptable and which are not. If you only want used or 100 percent recycled gifts, say so. Family members usually want to feel like they are being helpful and included, so find ways to make them part of your low-carbon lifestyle.

2. **Don't take criticism personally.** It's not always easy, but it is important to try to respond to criticism without being defensive. Do you ever fly to visit your family, or for work? Did

you crave bacon when you were pregnant? Are your shoes leather? If so, there are some people who will use those kinds of thing to discredit whatever actions you are taking to reduce your carbon footprint. Read up on the environmental impact of your choices and be ready to reword their question into ones that you are okay with answering. "It seems like what you're really trying to ask is, 'Are 100 percent of my choices the best for the environment?' It's a good question. I'd say it's more like 80 percent. Rather than try to do everything, I've prioritized the actions that are easiest for me to do and also have a large impact."

3. **Make your concerns personal.** Explain your personal passion for the issue as it relates to your concern for your baby. "I am a climate activist and I make the choices that I do because I fear for the future that my baby will inherit and I feel it is my job to protect my baby." It's much harder for people who love you to argue with a personal plea for understanding and support, so the more personal, and the less data-driven you make the conversation, the more likely they are to support you.

4. **Be willing to give a little.** If you really do not want a baby shower and your mother really wants to throw you a baby shower, try seeing if she is willing to organize a baby shower without new gifts. If you really want to use cloth diapers, but your husband finds them gross, be willing to let him diaper his way, while you diaper your way. If everyone thinks the baby must be cold with the heat so low, consider whether they have a point.

5. **Speak up, respectfully, on the big issues.** Deciding to move to a bigger or farther away house is a critical issue for your carbon footprint. So is deciding whether to buy an additional or fuel-guzzling car. It's likely that the person you are negotiating with has good intentions, but different priorities.

Prioritize the house and transportation decisions since they have the biggest impact. Find a way to respectfully convey why the decision at hand is so important to you, and try to find a compromise that gives some ground in other areas. For example, if your spouse is willing to let you get the most efficient car, consider letting him/her off the hook on changing cloth diapers.

During the first year of your baby's life, he or she will catch a cold at some point. He or she will also probably get diaper rash at some point. Unfortunately, the skeptics around you will use these occurrences as opportunities to undermine your efforts to reduce your carbon footprint. If your baby gets sick, some people will be eager to tell you that it is because your house is too cold, because you bought used toys that were dirty, or even because you didn't eat red meat during pregnancy. If your baby has diaper rash, your cloth diapers will be blamed, regardless of the fact that more rashes occur in babies wearing disposable diapers. Your baby isn't walking at twelve months? The answer will be to get him out of those cumbersome cloth diapers. Baby not sleeping? That too must be the fault of the cloth diapers. Not gaining weight fast enough? The first answer will be to drive to the store and buy some formula. You get the idea. Every single thing that goes wrong can and will be blamed on your efforts to reduce your carbon footprint. The good news is that the skeptics are probably wrong, as your actions are protecting your child in the long run by reducing pollution. Even more importantly, you are showing society that climate policies that bring about a different lifestyle need not be scary. In the end, your actions will help in securing a livable planet not only for your baby, but also for the babies of all those skeptics.

Form An Eco-Team

The more support you have as a new parent, the more likely you will be able to stick to your goal of reducing your carbon footprint. Breastfeeding, cloth diapering, elimination communication, and household carbon footprint reduction are all actions that are easier to engage if you are surrounded by people who believe as you do. To assist in keeping the skeptics at bay, and help make you more confident in the choices you are making for your baby, it is important to form a support group—i.e., an "eco-team." The concept is simple. You get together a group of people who are also interested in lowering their carbon footprint, and meet regularly so that you can lend support to one another. (A step-by-step guide for what your team can do at each gathering can be found in the book *The Low Carbon Diet* by David Gershon.[1]) Forming an "eco-team" is one of the most effective ways to spread the actions that will reduce your carbon footprint.

The first step in forming an "eco-team" is to think about who you know who might be open to reducing their carbon footprint. Identify five or six people who you are pretty sure would be up for this, and give each of them a call and ask if they'd be willing to get together weekly or monthly to talk about their efforts to reduce their carbon footprint. If you don't know five or six people who would be open to being on an "eco-team," try inviting your neighbors, and asking if they would like to join you in thinking through the things you can all do to help the environment. You can make it a "play date" of sorts and invite mostly new parents, or you can broaden the group to include anyone who is interested. You can start each meeting by talking about what you've accomplished since you last met, what barriers you faced, and how you were able to overcome those barriers. End the meeting with a discussion of your goals and aspirations for the coming weeks and what new changes you hope to implement or maintain.

If your "eco-team" really gels and is having fun meeting, consider expanding the scope of what you do in accordance with the interests of the group. You could start mixing in film or book discussions. The group may even want to consider getting together to brainstorm ideas for letters to the editor of your local paper, lobbying your local government or members of Congress, attending protests related to fossil fuels or climate change action, or even building alternative energy or food systems locally. If your group would like support from a broader effort, there are many local chapters of national efforts that you could also plug into, such as Citizen's Climate Lobby and Beyond Coal.

Coming Out Of The Climate Closet

In 2011, I attended a conference on climate change where a woman stood up and introduced herself by using a variation of the greeting used by members of Alcoholics Anonymous. "My name is Lisa," she said, "and I am a climate activist." She went on to say that she felt like talking to her family about why she was a climate activist parent had been harder than coming out of the closet. Her voice broke as she talked about how difficult it was for her to admit to her family that as a parent, climate change terrified her and had motivated her into action. She urged everyone in the room to find a way to make this issue personal and come out of the closet to all of our extended families.

After the conference, I approached Lisa and asked her a little more about what she had said. What was so frightening about talking to her family about climate change activism? What was she afraid of? She told me that what she feared was rejection, which is also what she feared when she had come out of the closet to her family. At that moment it occurred to me that although members of my family had come out, it was still taboo to talk about climate change with certain members of the family. As I spoke to more people at the conference about this climate silence, I found many who were scared to talk about their concerns about climate change. I had studied abroad in Spain when I was younger, and this situation reminded me a little of the human rights abuses that occurred under the Franco regime there. When neighbors disappeared, it was considered socially taboo and a bit rude to mention it to anybody. The abuses continued because of the silence. I realized then that the abuse of our planet would also continue until we broke the social taboo against talking about climate change.

After the conference, I started asking friends and colleagues about their experiences talking to their families about climate change, and found that almost no one had done it. Those who had tried had not managed to do so without getting into a fight. One friend had gotten into multiple arguments with her family about the science of climate change and didn't want to talk about it again. I talked to others who felt that it would be a rude topic to bring up. Still others assumed that their entire family agreed with them on the issue, so there was no reason to talk about it. I couldn't find anyone who spoke to their family on a regular basis about climate change. Everyone wanted to take the leap, though, so I got together with a few colleagues who wanted to talk about our concern for the future, what we were doing, and what others could do. It wasn't a traditional "eco-team," but the support and accountability helped everyone in the group take the next step with their families, and finally come out of the closet about our personal concerns about the planet our children would inherit.

Zero Footprint Options

Work through any fears you might have about admitting to your friends and family that you are scared about your baby's future because of the way that we are disrupting the Earth's climate. Make a resolution and a plan for when and how you will broach the conversation about climate change with your family. Working alone is hard because there's no accountability for sticking to whatever plan that you choose for yourself. That's why it is important to find partners in crime. Start an eco-team, and take charge of ensuring you have a support network. If you are nervous about starting your own group, plug yourself into local organizations that are already passionate about this issue like Citizen's Climate Lobby, or Beyond Coal. Have a plan in advance for holidays, birthdays, showers, and other events where friends and family will want to give you things. Turn those occasions into 'teachable moments' where you can speak from the heart about your fears and your motivations. Ask family members to only buy used or 100 percent recycled items and identify other ways for family members to show their love for your baby. Friends and family may not know that you value their time and love far more than any material items that they could purchase for you or your baby. Let them know.

10. Nap Time Activism

"I know how hard it is to find a moment for myself, much less for the whole world. But I also know that the whole world is what awaits my children."—Dominique Browning, founder of 'Mom's Clean Air Force'

The best (and most frequent) advice I got about being a new mom was to "sleep when the baby sleeps." The second best advice was to "keep going back to sleep in the morning, and stay in your pajamas until you get eight hours of sleep." Thanks to those two pieces of wisdom, after a few months, I felt composed enough to be able to set aside ten minutes a day to be a climate change activist. (I was eventually able to increase that time to thirty minutes a day because I found it so rewarding.) But can ten minutes a day really make a difference? And does anyone care what parents think about climate change policy? Luckily the answer to both questions is a resounding yes!

In this chapter, we will explore how parents with little time on their hands can work to advance national policies that tackle climate change, the most effective advocacy tools and efforts, and how much of an impact policy advocacy has in addressing environmental issues.

Ten Minutes To Save The World

We've all seen action films where the hero, with a bright red digital timer counting down the seconds, fights against time to save the world. Will he succeed before the clock hits zero, or will the world end? While it may not be quite as sexy or dramatic, in the amount of time that it takes to change a diaper, parents can save the world. Depending on the speed of your internet connection, even five minutes could be enough to make a real difference.

Here are some things you can do to fight for climate policies that won't take more than a few minutes of your day.

Contact Your Member Of Congress

In 2012, the research firm Englin Consulting interviewed congressional staff in order to find out which advocacy efforts from their constituents were most effective.[1] Three key findings stood out:

1. When it comes to Congress, all politics is still local. Members of Congress want to be re-elected every two years, which means they want to do things that will make their constituents want to re-elect them. Therefore, when contacting elected officials, only contact the ones that represent you or your district. Elected officials care what their constituents think—but not what others who can't vote for them do.

2. You need to make the right ask at the right time. That means naming the specific bill you are concerned about and indicating which way you want your elected representative to vote. If there is no bill to vote on, your call or email should be linked to a catalytic event that will make elected officials interested in climate change, like Hurricane Sandy in 2012. The best way to know what is going on is to join advocacy organizations that can do the homework for you and alert you to opportunities to advance climate change policy.

3. Quality trumps quantity for Congress. A personalized email is more powerful than just filling in the form email in the way suggested by an organization. A caller who is able to articulate why climate change worries them as a new par-

ent, how a specific extreme weather event effected them, and what they are doing in their own lives to make a difference is much more effective than hundreds of calls parroting stock talking points. Letters to the editor of the local paper can also make a difference. The best way to have an effect is to make an appointment to visit your local representative in their home office, and to bring some friends along with you if possible for a conversation about climate change.

When speaking of what actions have the most influence on elected officials, the chief of staff of one member of congress put it this way, "If you had a rally with 500 people at the State House and it showed up in the [state paper] the next day, then that is important. If you had five hundred people send a form letter on a generic issue, I would say that is less important. If you had fifty people calling from the district on a particular issue, I would say that would be better."[2] This shows how important it is to coordinate your actions with other local activists—whether it is to show up at the State House, make a call or send an email on the same day.

In addition, attending a rally that is aimed at garnering local media attention is an excellent way to influence your elected officials. While it will definitely take longer than ten minutes, the good thing is that many rallies are very baby-friendly. Although there is often a stage, it's not like attending the theater—nobody minds if your baby starts crying and there are usually plenty of patches of grass available for changing a diaper.

Our Protest Story

Five days after our son was born in 2010, we took him to the Rally to Restore Sanity that Jon Stewart was holding on the National Mall in Washington DC. I could barely walk at the time, so we had to borrow a wheelchair. I strapped the baby into a sling carrier, got in the wheelchair, and my husband Andrew pushed us both to a rally of over 200,000 people demanding a civil discourse as part of our democracy. It was actually fun to get priority treatment and sit in the wheelchair section right in front of the stage. I realized that day that rallies were events that the whole family could enjoy together.

As a result of that positive experience, when my son was eleven months old, I initially had no hesitation when I heard that protestors were going to the White House to rally against the Keystone XL pipeline that was designed to bring the dirtiest of dirty energy, tar sands, from Canada down to the Gulf Coast for export. However, I did have some trepidation when I found out that, inspired by the courageous acts of non-violence during the civil rights movement and the non-violent civil disobedience that had won freedom for India, the plan was for everyone at the rally to get arrested. The organizers had brought together an impressive group of people who were willing to get arrested in order to stop the pipeline, including several well-known celebrities and the former dean of the Duke University School of the Environment.

When I spoke to the organizers about my fears, they said that most people at the protest would be like me—people who had never come close to being arrested and prided themselves on being law-abiding citizens. They said we would all be charged with a misdemeanor, a minor infraction that wouldn't even appear on our records. They told me it would only take two hours or so to get processed, but admitted that if the police wanted to make a point, they could keep us overnight. I was still nursing at the time, and wasn't sure how that would work if I got arrested. The organizers told me they had no idea how the DC police would handle a nursing mother, and encouraged me to find out more information if I was so inclined.

I called the police and asked what their policies were for nursing mothers who were arrested. How long could a nursing mother be held, for example? There was no time limit, I discovered.

Would they allow me to pump milk with an electric breast pump? No, was the answer. What if a mom needed to hand express milk, would they provide any containers? No. If someone else brought the baby, could the mother nurse it? They didn't know because it had never happened. I called back the event organizers and they strongly encouraged me not to get arrested with the rest of the protestors based on the information I had found out. They didn't want news stories about how badly lactating mothers were treated by the police when they were in the early days of trying to get the media to take notice of the damage that would be caused by the pipeline. However, they invited me to come along to offer support to the rest of the protesters.

The following day, I put Siddharth in his baby carrier and headed to the White House for the protest. I went with a group of protestors to the "picture area" in front of the building, and when we had been there for a few minutes longer than allowed by law, the police formed a barricade around us with only one exit and told us that we needed to leave through that exit in an orderly fashion. Speaking through a bullhorn, an officer yelled out instructions. "I will give you three warnings in total, and then we will begin arresting all of you." Two police officers on my side were shooting me pleading looks, and waving toward the exit—a woman carrying a baby was really not what they wanted to deal with that morning. I was getting a little anxious myself, but stayed another ten minutes until the second warning was announced. I then excused myself and made my way toward the exit. The police officers let me out, clearly thrilled that they would not have to deal with arresting a mother and child. I thanked them for their hard work as I walked by.

After I exited the barricade, I met up with a friend and her baby and my sister in the park in front of the White House where we had a small picnic lunch while expressing support to the protesters as the police went through the slow process of arresting everyone and putting them on buses. I felt bad that my friends had taken such courageous action and gotten themselves arrested to protect my son's future while I sat on the sidelines. On the other hand, I was proud of the role I had played in highlighting who the victims of the pipeline would be—our children, and their children.

A Step By Step Guide to Influencing Your Member of Congress

Not everyone will want to get arrested to fight climate change, even if it is for the sake of their children's future. However, you don't have to go that far. In ten minutes a day, you can make a difference right from your home. In order for your ten minutes of advocacy to be most effective, a little preparation can go a long way.

- Get the phone number and email address for the local office of your member of congress.

- Find out what their position is on climate change. You can do this by skimming their website (which will also help you understand their background, priorities, and what kind of arguments will resonate with them most). You can also type their name into the League of Conservation Voters website and click on the detailed report to see how they voted on climate change bills. You can also visit the website www.dirtyenergymoney.com to find out how much money they take from the fossil fuel industry.

- Sign up with an advocacy group that will alert you to opportunities for action. One that is geared towards parents is Mom's Clean Air Forc (www.momscleanairforce. org). You can also join national organizations that work on a variety of issues including climate change, such as World Wildlife Fund, Greenpeace, Sierra Club, Natural Resource Defense Council, Environmental Defense Fund, and Earth Justice. You can either follow them on social media sites like Twitter or Facebook, or sign up for email alerts. You can sign up for all of them, or just one to begin with. The key is to know when the moment is ripe for your phone call, email, or visit to your elected official.

- Think about what will move your member of Congress. Is your representative a progressive champion who always votes the right way but never introduces climate legislation or talks about it publicly? If so, you should focus your messages on asking not only for votes but for more public statements about climate change and new legislation. Even the progressive members of Congress need to hear more from their constituents about climate change. Is your representative a Tea Party follower who does not believe that humans cause climate change? In that case, focus on your personal story. Explain how worrying about climate change affects you as a parent, tell them what you are doing in your own life to help fight it, and how you need their help on this issue as your representative in Congress.

What Happens When You Call Your Elected Representative?

When you call your senator or member of Congress during office hours, an intern will often answer the phone. You should tell them "Hi my name is _____. I am a constituent, and I am calling to support action on climate change." They will ask if there is a specific bill you are calling about, and if so, take down the name of that bill. If they know it already, they might tell you the member's position on the bill or issue without you asking for it. If not, you can ask about their position. Take a moment to tell them why you are concerned about climate change as a new parent and tell a story about what you are doing in your personal life. Say that you are doing all that you can, but you really need help from your member of Congress to protect your baby. After you hang up, the person who answered the phone will note the topic of your call, and the total tally of topics people called about will be presented to the senator/congresswoman at the start of the next day. The topics that most people call about will usually get the most attention. The more personal your story is, the more likely it will be conveyed to the official. To be most effective, use your call to also schedule a meeting in the local office with a staff member. You can bring your baby to the meeting if you need to. My sister-in-law is a midwife and usually has one of her babies with her when she visits congressional staff. In some ways, it is better to bring your baby because it will help the staff remember you. If possible, bring friends along who have their own compelling stories. Ask the staff member questions and get to know them on a personal level. Constituents who know the staff of their members of Congress can make a big difference.

The Numbers: How Much Pollution Can Be Reduced By A Climate Crusader?

In the previous chapters, I calculated the carbon pollution savings of taking actions that lead to a zero footprint baby for the first year. It's harder to do the same thing with climate policies, but just to give you a sense of scale, I'll attempt it.

For the sake of argument, let's take a hypothetical situation where you are one of a 100 people in a congressional district who are able to convince your member of Congress to support a suite of national climate change policies (e.g. renewable energy, additional regulation of greenhouse gases, a carbon tax swap, a cap and trade system). I am then further assuming that the policy that you achieve has the effect of reducing emissions in one year by 150 million metric tons of CO_2e, which is around what would have been achieved by the "Waxman-Markey" climate bill that passed the House of Representatives but not the Senate in 2009.[3]

For this hypothetical situation, I'm going to imagine that you live in South Florida, where home values have already been affected by the rise of the ocean, which results in storm surges coming further inland. In 2009, only one of the congressional representatives in South Florida voted for climate policy, despite the clear effects of sea level rise on their communities. In our scenario, we'll assume you changed all that. You organized presentations from climate scientists from the local university to show maps of sea level rise in the district, as well as from local university economists who understood the impacts of the new policies, small business owners who had experienced more floods, parent groups worried about their homes having lost value, and key donors to the congressional member, all in order to make your case. This effort takes several years, and hundreds of hours of your time. It also means that you have to pay for the occasional meal for meetings at your house, and for printing of materials, perhaps a couple thousand dollars total, but possibly higher if you cater the meals, or pay for experts to attend your meetings.

We'll also assume that similar people interested in climate change exist in other congressional districts, and that over half of them were also successful in their efforts. For the sake of simplicity I'll say that each member of Congress or Senator who votes for the bill is responsible for 1/535 of the solution (this isn't exactly right, since senators are more powerful than members of the House, and the voting rules are different for each body. Also, you wouldn't need all of the votes to get the bill passed, but this is just an exercise). Your actions are 1/100 of 1/535 of the solution. Since the new carbon policies reduce emissions by 150 million metric tons in one year, your member of Congress is responsible for about 280,000 tons of pollution reduction. As one of the 100 people who did the most to change that member's mind, you would personally be responsible for a hundredth of those reductions, or 2,800 tons of carbon reduction.

In reality, this is a difficult thing to calculate for many reasons. First, it's hard to determine how many people it takes to make a difference in changing policy, though we do know that members of Congress and their staff listen to their constituents. We also know that millions of dollars in ads from the fossil fuel industry haven't done much to improve their image in this country, so perhaps we could win even without the resources to counter their newspaper, radio, and TV advertisement. It's not easy, but it is possible. In fact, it happened in 2009 when the "Waxman-Markey" climate bill passed in the House of Representatives; it just didn't make it through the Senate that time. Still, the nice thing about taking personal and political action is that you can be sure the personal action makes a difference, and you know that the political action could have a big payoff. One is low risk, with definite reward, while the other is high risk, high reward. The ideal type of activity is low risk, high reward, but there are few actions that fall into that category when it comes to climate change activism.

What Could Our Children's Future Look Like?

If we succeed in passing policies that dramatically affect climate change, like putting a tax on carbon, our children will live in a far different world than we do today. In that future world, utility bills will be low because it will take very little power to heat and cool our energy efficient homes. We'll be healthier because we will have the option to walk, bike, and take public transportation wherever we go. People will live in transit-oriented communities, and those with cars will own electric vehicles that are powered by the sun and the wind. As a matter of fact, all of our daily activities will be powered by the sun and the wind—from washing our clothes to cooking our food. Our food will be cheaper and better for us because we will grow it in our own gardens, or buy it from local farms or farmer's markets. Asthma rates for our grandchildren will be lower because air quality will improve, and we will have plans in place to cope with any increase in heat waves. In short, we will have protected the Earth for another generation, and will pass along to our children a planet where they can live and thrive.

Zero Footprint Options

Changing government policies can potentially have an even bigger impact than all the other actions that you take to reduce your carbon footprint. It takes time to influence policy, but if you can find even ten minutes a day for "nap time activism," it can make a difference, especially if it is in chorus with thousands of other parents who are also taking a few minutes a day to weigh in. The key to making a difference is to be active with your local elected officials. Once you learn more about him or her and their positions, you can develop a plan for turning that individual into a champion for climate change policies, or you can find out what plans are in the works locally. Groups like Citizen's Climate Lobby often have plans in place for influencing their member of Congress locally, and organizations such as Mom's Clean Air Force specifically rally parents to become climate change policy advocates. Everything won't change within the first year of your baby's life, but it can happen over the course of a few years. If you succeed, you will have done your job as a parent by doing everything you could to protect the future of the planet for your child.

Epilogue: Our Zero Footprint Baby

I'll end any lingering suspense right now: my husband and I did have a zero footprint baby in the first year! In fact, our emissions were a lot lower in the first year of Siddharth's life than they had been in previous years when there had been just the two of us. Although the current estimates of the cost of a child are $13,050 per year, we found that with our new bundle of joy in the house, we didn't actually spend much money at all.[1] Having a baby mostly meant not doing as much of the things that usually cost money—like going out or traveling. At the end of the first year, we had saved both money and carbon emissions.

After all my research on natural birth, diapers, breastfeeding, and efficient refrigeration for breast milk, we were able to prevent our carbon footprint from going up in those areas. The real trick was finding a place to cut emissions. Since we felt we had to buy a refrigerator and start using heat and air conditioning, we needed to find something big to offset that increased usage. We had already insulated our house, installed solar panels, and an efficient air handler, and we had long ago ditched our car. But the one thing we hadn't cut back on yet was our air travel. To address the pollution from travel, we began to take the train or bus whenever we could. We vacationed closer to home, and even missed a few weddings of friends and family. The tradeoff was that the reduction in our pollution was enormous. (In the interest of full disclosure, our carbon footprint before and after our baby are included in the book's appendix, as well as a comparison of the carbon footprint reduction from different actions.) While we may be unique in where the fat in our carbon budget was—I'm guessing not many people take multiple international flights each year—everyone has some area where their carbon footprint is high. For some people it is their heating or air conditioning; for others it is their daily commute, or their consumption. Nearly everyone in this country has a fair amount they can cut from their carbon budgets.

It felt good at the end of the year to have reduced our carbon budget. And the process of reducing our carbon footprint was so simple that it gave me more confidence than ever that we can solve this problem on a society-wide level. It also made me optimistic about my son's future, and this renewed optimism allowed me to focus on the politics of renewable energy. After the year we spent working toward our zero carbon baby, I feel even better about the prospects of engaging other parents in the quest for carbon neutral homes, carbon neutral communities, and eventually, a carbon neutral nation and world.

I am now in a very different position from the pregnant woman who was desperately collecting used baby gear from friends. Now I am the one who is eager to get rid of baby clothes as quickly as possible in order to make room for clothes that actually fit my child. I am the one looking for someone in my office or neighborhood who will fit into my maternity clothes and take my baby clothes. As my son grows older, I find myself having fun telling him who gave him different articles of clothing and even finding pictures of my friends' children wearing the clothes that are now in his closet. I also try to give him a chance to be a part of giving his clothes away to a smaller baby, and find that he loves the idea that a little baby will one day wear his things. As an older child, I can also now help him understand which plants his food and clothing come from.

I think, and hope, that my child will inevitably see the world differently because of the way he was raised as a baby. Sometimes, this will bring up big questions, and I will have to be ready to offer answers in a way that does not frighten my child, but rather makes him feel secure that he is being taken care of. I'm already seeing that he will also do certain things naturally, like be reluctant to throw things into the trash that could possibly be recycled or reused, or be willing to treasure a found item from the street.

One of the major issues that I dread is the amount of advertizing and peer pressure to consume that my child will face in the coming years. In the first few years of his life, avoiding television solved the problem of commercialism and consumerism, but that can only last so long. Eventually, Siddharth will ask for the toys that other children have, and feel isolated when he does not have certain things that his friends have. I have already found myself wondering if I am doing the right thing when faced with his pleading for certain toys or clothes. More than once, I have asked myself the question, "Am I depriving my child of something that he would benefit from developmentally?" At those moments, I have to remind myself that the questions we all have to face as a society is not if it is fair for our children to have fewer toys and international trips and smaller cars., but instead, do we have the right to imperil the future of the planet that our children and their children will inherit? If we, as parents, don't solve this problem now, who will? If we don't do it right now, then when will it be done?

The answer is that we can't afford to wait until it is too late.

Resources

Rather than provide websites that may change, I've provided the names of organizations or programs to enable internet searches.

Activism
Mom's Clean Air Force

Citizen's Climate Lobby

Climate Parents

WWF's Conservation Action Network

Efficient Appliances
Sunfrost Refrigerators

TopTenUSA

Energy Star

SinkPositive

Renewable Energy
Green Power Network' operated by the Department of Energy

Real Estate

Green Building Council, LEED program

ECObroker or ECO Real Estate certification

Birth
The American College of Nurse Midwives

The Midwives Alliance of North America

Baby Gear
Craigslist

Ebay

kidsstuffsale.com

Diaperswappers

ThredUp

Breastfeeding

Kelly Mom

Hygeia pumps

Elimination Communication/Cloth Diapers

"Diaper free baby"

Nellie's laundry soda

BumGenius

FuzziBunz

Appendix 1—Our Carbon Footprint

Category	Pre-baby annual CO2 emitted (lbs)	With baby annual CO2 emitted (lbs)	Difference	Notes
Work-place emissions	1252	1043	-209	I was not at work for 4 months in the first year. (Also, I counted these emissions despite that half of these emissions are 'offset' by my employer, meaning that they fund emissions reductions elsewhere at the scale of the pollution they create. My husband's employer does not offset.)
Work-place travel emissions	5551+ 2125+ 2303+ 516+ 4001+ 1997= 16,493	0	-16,493	Bangkok (x2), Barcelona, Copenhagen, Atlanta, India (x2), Bonn in 2010. (Only one flight to Bangkok and one to India were not offset, because my employer offsets all flights). No trips in 2011; Used my baby as an excuse not to travel and used video conference in place of three planned trips. Had no planned trips during maternity leave.
House-hold energy	0	0	281	We have solar panels and selected 100% wind energy halfway through 2011 to cover the rest. Since we knew we'd be using appliances more, we got the most efficient dish-washer, washing machine, air handler, and refrigerator available in 2011. We did need additional energy using more heating and a/c than we did before the baby.
House-hold food consump-tion	2920	3285	365	4kWh/day for a vegetarian diet. Baby-related increase was due to increased calories during nursing and solids in the last 6 months, equivalent to 1kWh/day.[1]
House-hold consump-tion	16,000	16,000	0	This category includes any new clothing, electronics, gifts, personal care products, health care (including birth), and other merchandise. The only new items were a nursing bra and two gifts—a crib and a few out-fits. The consumption was the same as the previous year.

Category	Pre-baby annual CO2 emitted (lbs)	With baby annual CO2 emitted (lbs)	Difference	Notes
Personal local transportation	2,200	2,200	0	Three vacation trips each year to West Virginia, Delaware, and Charlottesville. Monthly local family visit to Fairfax, Fredericksburg, or Baltimore. Metro on weekends and non-biking/running commuting days. No measureable difference with the baby.
Personal flights	0	1272	1272	San Diego in 2011. We made one personal trip to visit friends in San Diego for a special occasion.
Family share of municipal/state emissions	9248	13872	4624	Source: District of Columbia Greenhouse Gas Emissions Inventories and Preliminary Projections, District of Columbia Department of Health, Air Quality Division, 2005.
Family share of Federal Government Emissions	1122	1683	561	These emissions are almost all DOD. While emissions barely changed between years, we took on the share for three people in the second year.[2]
Family share of internet servers	392	588	196	The computer-servers in US data centers and their associated plumbing (air conditioners, backup power systems, and so forth) consumed 0.4 kWh per day per person—just over 1% of US electricity consumption.[3]
Total			-9403	**Officially a -9403 lbs CO2 baby! That's less than zero!** (This does not even include our offsetting of our entire footprint for 2011 using Gold Standard Offsets.)

Appendix 2: Comparison of carbon pollution reduction of various actions

Example actions taken to save CO2 in the first year of a baby's life	CO2 saved in one year (metric tons)	Upfront Personal Cost for one year (USD)	Time commitment
Used onesies instead of new[1]	0.06	(-$100)	1 hour per month
Used cloth diapers that are line dried vs. disposables or new cloth diapers with a clothes dryer[2]	0.15	(-$900)	3 hours per week
Replace refrigerator with energy-efficient model[3]	0.25	$2,000	3 hours—one time
Home retrofit, or moving to a home that is 20% more efficient[4]	1.6	$5,000-$15,000	3 months—one time
Breastfeeding with additional calories from lentils vs lamb*	2.5	(-$500)	N/A—no extra time
Avoid two cross-country plane trips for two sets of grandparents (by living close by or reduced visits)[5]	2.6	(-$3,000)	3 months (moving)—one time
Natural birth at home instead of C-Section*	4	(-$12,000)	10 hours (research)
Reduce miles driven from 240 to 50 per week, assuming 20 mpg[6]	4.6	(-$1,800)	1 hour daily for non-car commute; 3 months to move to transit oriented home
Switch to 100% green energy[7]	8	$215	30 minutes—one time
Trade in GM Yukon with 12 mpg for Prius with 50 mpg[8]	9	$0	3 hours—one time
Fertile couple adopting locally[9]	20	$0-$2,500	1 year
Convincing your member of Congress to support a national climate policy that becomes law	2,800	$2000-$200,000	Multiple years; hundreds of hours per year

* CO2 saved calculations are explained in the text of the relevant chapter

ACKNOWLEDGEMENTS

I cannot come up with words that convey how grateful I am for the patience and love of my husband and my son, and the support of our families. I also want to thank my agent, Diana Finch, for guiding me through this process, and reviewing so many early drafts. Many dear friends from many walks of life also put their time and energy into helping me with this project, including Brian Levy, Alexandra Levit, Heidi Coryell Williams, Kathleen Feeney Chappell, Kristine O'Brien Redlien, and Deborah Lawrence.

NOTES

Introduction

1. US Global Change Research Program, *Global Climate Change Impacts in the US*, Thomas R. Karl, Jerry M. Melillo, and Thomas C. Peterson (eds.), (Cambridge University Press, 2009), http://www.globalchange. gov/publications/reports/scientific-assessments/us-impacts.com

2. Tony Dutzik, Elizabeth Ridlington and Tom Van Heeke, Frontier Group and Nathan Willcox, "In the Path of the Storm: Global Warming, Extreme Weather and the Impacts of Weather-Related Disasters in the United States from 2007 to 2012," Environment America Research & Policy Center, 2012.

3. James Hansena, Makiko Satoa, and Reto Ruedy, "Perception of climate change," *Proceedings of the National Academy of Sciences* (August 6, 2012): 1-9, http://www.pnas.org/cgi/doi/10.1073/pnas.1205276109.

1. Building Your Nest

1. Stephanie J Battles and Eugene M Burns, "Trends in Building-Related Energy and Carbon Emissions: Actual and Alternate Scenarios Sector," *Energy and Envrionmental Policy* 9, no. 1 (1998): 1-12; United Nations Environment Programme, Buildings and Climate Change (Paris, 2007).

2. World Resources Institute, "Climate Analysis Indicators Tool (CAIT)", 2009, http://www.wri.org/project/cait/.

3. Shahzeen Z. Attaria, Michael L. DeKayb, Cliff I. Davidsonc, and Wändi Bruine de Bruin, "Public Perceptions of Energy Consumption and Savings," *Proceedings of the National Academy of Sciences of the United States of America* 107, no. 37 (September 14, 2010): 16054-9.

4. U.S. Energy Information Administration, "Share of Energy

Used by Appliances and Consumer Electronics Increases in U.S. homes," Residential Energy Consumption Survey (RECS), 2012, http://205.254.135.7/consumption/residential/reports/electronics. cfm.

5. United States Census Bureau, "2010 Census", 2010, http://2010.census.gov/2010census/.

6. U.S. Energy Information Administration, "Residential Energy Consumption Survey: The impact of increasing home size on energy demand," Residential Energy Consumption Survey (RECS)—Analysis & Projections, 2012, http://205.254.135.7/consumption/residential/reports/2009-square-footage.cfm.

7. U.S. Department of Energy, *Energy Efficiency Trends in Residential and Commercial Buildings* (Washington, DC, 2008).

8. David Dodman, "Blaming Cities for Climate Change? An Analysis of Urban Greenhouse Gas Emissions Inventories," *Environment and Urbanization* 21, no. 1 (April 1, 2009): 185-201, http://eau.sagepub.com/cgi/content/abstract/21/1/185.

9. Jukka Heinonen and Seppo Junnila, "Implications of urban structure on carbon consumption in Metropolitan areas," *Environmental Research Letters* 6, no. 1 (January 1, 2011): 1-9.

10. Elizabeth Kolbert, "The Island in the Wind," *New Yorker*, July 7, 2008.

11. Shanti Pless, Lynn Billman, Daniel Wallach, "From Tragedy to Triumph: Rebuilding Greensburg, Kansas, To Be a 100 % Renewable Energy City," ACEEE Summer Study on Energy Efficiency in Buildings, 2010.

12. Daniel Hernandez, Matthew Lister, and Celine Suarez, "Location Efficiency and Housing Type: Boiling it Down to BTU's", *Land Use Tracker* 10, no. 4 (Spring 2011).

13. Mark A Schipper, "Household Vehicles Energy Use: Latest Data & Trends," Energy Information Administration, vol. 0464 (Washington, DC, 2005).

2. Prenatal Care and the Birth of Your Child

1.R. Barakat, M. Pelaez, C. Lopez, R. Montejo, and J. Coteron, "Exercise During Pregnancy Reduces the Rate of Cesarean and Instrumental Deliveries: Results of a Randomized Controlled Trial," *Journal of Maternal-fetal and Neonatal Medicine*, 25(11), 2372–6; J. Dempsey, C. Butler, and M. Williams, "No Need for a Pregnant Pause: Physical Activity May Reduce the Occurrence of Gestational Diabetes Mellitus and Preeclampsia," *Exercise and Sport Science Reviews* 2, 33(3), 141–149.

2. Toni Meier and Olaf Christen, "Gender as a factor in an environmental assessment of the consumption of animal and plant-based foods in Germany, " *International Journal of Life Cycle Assessment* 17, no. 5 (June 2012), 550–564.

3. American Dietetic Association, "Position of the American Dietetic Association: Vegetarian Diets," *Journal of the American Dietetic Association* 109, no. 7 (July 2009) 1266–1282.

4. J.W Chung and D.O. Meltzer, "Estimate of the Carbon Footprint of the US Healthcare Sector," *JAMA: The Journal of the American Medical Association* 302, no. 18 (November 2009): 2009-2011.

5. U.S. Government Accountability Office, Reprocessed Single-Use Medical Devies: FDA Oversight Has Increased, and Available Information Does Not Indicate That Use Presents an Elevated Health Risk, January 2008, (p. 38).

6. US Energy Information Administration, "Electricity in the United States: Energy Explained, Your Guide To Understanding Energy," 2011.

7. Chung and Meltzer, "Estimate of the Carbon Footprint of the US Healthcare Sector.."

8. World Resources Institute, "Climate Analysis Indicators Tool," 2009, http://www.wri.org/project/cait/ (accessed June 5, 2012).

9. Thomson Healthcare, "The Healthcare Costs of Having a Baby," June 2007.

10. R E Anderson and D A Anderson, "The Cost-Effectiveness of Home Birth," *Journal of Nurse-Midwifery* 44, 30–5.

11. American College of Nurse-Midwives, Midwifery: Evidence-Based Practice: A Summary of Research on Midwifery Practice in the United States, April 2012.

12. Henci Goer, *The Thinking Woman's Guide to a Better Birth* (New York: Perigee, 1999).

13. Penny Simkin, *The Birth Partner, Third Edition: A Complete Guide to*

Childbirth for Dads, Doulas, and All Other Labor Companions (Boston: Harvard Common Press, 2008).

3. All That Baby Gear

1. Denise Fields, *Baby Bargains, 8th Edition: Secrets to Saving 20% to 50% on Baby Furniture, Gear, Clothes, Toys, Maternity Wear and Much, Much More!* (Boulder, CO: Windsor Peak Press, 2010).
2. Eric Clark, *The Real Toy Story: Inside the Ruthless Battle for America's Youngest Consumers* (New York: Free Press, 2007).
3. Mike Berners-Lee, *How Bad Are Bananas?: The Carbon Footprint of Everything* (Canada: Greystone Books, 2011).
4. Brian Palmer, "It's Smart to Reuse Baby Items, Aside from Breast-milk Pumps and Car Seats," *Slate*, July 17, 2011, http://www.washingtonpost.com/wp-dyn/content/article/2011/01/17/AR2011011702954.html.
5. Wee-Sale Pricing Guidelines, http://www.wee-sale.com/Pricing_Guidelines.pdf
6. Ibid.
7. Clark, *The Real Toy Story: Inside the Ruthless Battle for America's Youngest Consumers.*
8. Susan Linn, *Consuming Kids: The Hostile Takeover of Childhood* (New York: The New Press, 2004).
9. National Institutes of Health, "Screen time and children," *MedlinePlus Medical Encyclopedia*, 2011, http://www.nlm.nih.gov/medlineplus/ency/patientinstructions/000355.htm.
10. U.S. Energy Information Administration, "Share of energy used by appliances and consumer electronics increases in U.S. homes," Residential Energy Consumption Survey, 2012, http://205.254.135.7/consumption/residential/reports/electronics.cfm.
11. Campaign for a Commercial-Free Childhood, "Baby Scam: Marketing to Infants and Toddlers."
12. World Wildlife Fund, Living Planet Report 2012.
13. Ming Xu, Ran Li, John Crittenden, Yongsheng Chen., "CO_2 emissions embodied in China's exports from 2002 to 2008: A structural decomposition analysis," *Energy Policy* 39, no. 11 (November 2011): 7381-7388.

4. Are Cloth Diapers A "Clothian" Bargain?

1. Carlos Richer, "Disposable Diaper History," Disposable Diaper Industry Source, http://disposablediaper.net/general-information/disposable-diaper-history/.
2. Environmental Protection Agency, Municipal Solid Waste Generation, Recycling, and Disposal in the United States in 2010, 2011.
3. Christine Gross-Loh, *The Diaper-Free Baby: The Natural Toilet Training Alternative* (New York: William Morrow, 2007).
4. Jana McKenzie, "Greenhouse Gas Footprint of Maintained Landscapes," Sustainable Design and Development Blog, June 2010, http://sustainableppn.asla.org/2010/06/08/greenhouse-gas-footprint-of-maintained-landscapes/.
5. Kate O'Brien, Rachel Olive, Yu-Chieh Hsu, Luke Morris, Richard Bell and Nick Kendall , "Life Cycle Assessment: reusable and disposable nappies in Australia," in Australian Life Cycle Assessment Society Conference 2009, *6th Australian Conference on Life Cycle Assessment, Melbourne,* (1-14). 17-19 February.
6. Simon Aumonier, Michael Collins, and Peter Garrett, *An updated lifecycle assessment study for disposable and reusable nappies* (Bristol: Environment Agency: 2008).

5. Feeding the Beast (Baby)

1. Centers for Disease Control and Prevention, Breastfeeding Report Card—United States, 2011.
2. Jan Riordan and Karen Wambach, *Breastfeeding and Human Lactation, Fourth Edition* (Subury, MA: Jones & Bartlett Publishers, 2009).
3. Jennifer L. Baker, Michael Gamborg, Berit L. Heitmann, Lauren Lissner, Thorkild IA Sørensen, and Kathleen M Rasmussen, "Breastfeeding Reduces Postpartum Weight Retention," *American Journal of Clinical Nutrition* 88, no. 6 (2008), 1–4.
4. Kari Hamerschlag, Meat Eater's Guide to Climate Change and Health, Environmental Working Group, September 2011, 25.
5. Michael Pollan, *In Defense of Food: An Eater's Manifesto* (New York: Penguin, 2008).
6. Food and Drug Administration, "Powdered Infant Formula: An

Overview of Manufacturing Processes," http://www.fda.gov/ohrms/
dockets/ac/03/briefing/3939b1_tab4b.htm [accessed 8 June 2012].

7. Hamerschlag, 25.

8. Jorgelina Pasqualino, Montse Meneses and Francesc Castells, "The Carbon Footprint and Energy Consumption of Beverage Packaging Selection and Disposal," *Journal of Food Engineering* 103 (2011), 357–365.

9. Ashok Chapagain and Keith James, "The Water and Carbon Footprint of Household Food and Drink Waste in the UK: A Report Containing Quantification and Analysis of the Water and Carbon", Waste & Resources Action Programme, 2011.

10. Environmental Protection Agency, "Municipal Solid Waste Generation, Recycling, and Disposal in the United States in 2010, 2011."

11. Jonathan Bloom, *American Wasteland: How America Throws Away Nearly Half of Its Food (and What We Can Do About It)*, (New York: Da Capo Lifelong Books, 2010).

6. The Child Care Dilemma

1. International Labour Organization, "Maternity Protection at Work," International Labour Conference 87th Session, Report V, I, 1999, http://www.ilo.org/public/english/standards/relm/ilc/ilc87/rep-v-1.htm#Maternity leave> [accessed 7 December 2012].

2. US Census Bureau, Survey of Income and Program Participation, Child, 2011.

3. Environmental Protection Agency, Greenhouse Gas Emissions from a Typical Passenger Vehicle, December 2011.

7. Family Size: How Much Is Too Much?

1. Gallup, "Small Families Are Most Americans' Ideal," March 29, 2004.

2. Gallup, "Children: What do you think is the ideal number of children for a family to have?," http://www.gallup.com/poll/1588/children-violence.aspx

3. World Wildlife Fund, "Living Planet Report," 2012.

4. Paul A. Murtaugh and Michael G. Schlax, "Reproduction and the carbon legacies of individuals," *Global Environmental Change* 19, no. 1 (February 2009): 14-20.

5. Steven Sherwood and Matthew Huber, "An Adaptabiity Limit to Climate Change Due to Heat Stress," Proceedings of the National Academy of Sciences, 2010.

6. World Resources Institute, "Climate Analysis Indicators Tool," 2009, http://www.wri.org/project/cait/, (accessed 5 June 2012).

7. Seth Borenstein, "Climate Change: Arctic Passes 400 Parts Per Million Milestone," *Christian Science Monitor*, May 31, 2012, http://www.csmonitor.com/Science/2012/0531/Climate-change-Arctic-passes-400-parts-per-million-milestone.

8. Tara Bahrampour, "U.S. birthrate plummets to its lowest level since 1920," *Washington Post*, November 19, 2012.

9. Mark Mather, "What's Driving the Decline in U.S. Population Growth?," Population Reference Bureau, May 2012, http://www.prb.org/Articles/2012/us-population-growth-decline.aspx.

10. *BBC News*, "Germany Stages Anti-nuclear Marches After Fukushima," March 26, 2011, http://www.bbc.co.uk/news/world-europe-12872339.

11. *The Economist*, "Germany's Energy Transformation: Energiewende," July 28, 2012, http://www.economist.com/node/21559667.

12. CleanTechnica, "Germany—26% of Electricity From Renewable Energy During First Half of 2012," July 26, 2012, http://cleantechnica.com/2012/07/26/germany-26-of-electricity-from-renewable-energy-in-1st-half-of-2012/ (accessed 28 December 2012).

13. Toni Falbo and Denise F. Polit, "Quantitative Review of the Only Child Literature: Research Evidence and Theory Development," *Psychological Bulletin* 100, no. 2 (1986), 176-189.

14. Karen Segboer, "I don't have kids: deal with it," *New York Times*, June 20, 2011, http://cityroom.blogs.nytimes.com/2011/06/20/complaint-box-i-dont-have-kids-deal-with-it/

8. The Adoption Option

1. U.S. Department of Health and Human Services, Administration for Children and Families, Children in Public Foster Care Who Are Waiting to Be Adopted FY 2003–FY 2011.

2. Dave Thomas Foundation for Adoption, "National Foster Care Adoption Attitudes Survey: Executive Summary," November 2007, http://

www.davethomasfoundation.org/wp-content/uploads/2011/02/ExecSummary_NatlFosterCareAdoptionAttitudesSurvey.pdf

3. U.S. Department of Health and Human Services, Child Welfare Information Gateway, "How Many Children Were Adopted in 2007 and 2008 ?," 2011.

4. International Civil Aviation Organization, "ICAO Carbon Emissions Calculator," http://www2.icao.int/en/carbonoffset/Pages/default.aspx

5. World Resources Institute, "Climate Analysis Indicators Tool," 2009, http://www.wri.org/project/cait/ (accessed June 5, 2012).

6. 'China Adoption Forecast—Updated January 5, 2012, http://chinaadoptionforecast.com/

7. Kelly Mom, "Notes from "Induced Lactation and Adoptive Nursing," 1999, http://kellymom.com/bf/got-milk/adoptivebf/.

8. David Biello, "Human Population Reaches 7 Billion—How Did This Happen and Can It Go On?," *Scientific American*, October 27, 2011, http://www.scientificamerican.com/article.cfm?id=human-population-reaches-seven-billion.

9. Bringing Others On Board

1. David Gershon, *Low Carbon Diet: A 30 Day Program to Lose 5000 Pounds—Be Part of the Global Warming Solution!* (Woodstock, NY: Empowerment Institute, 2006).

10. Nap Time Activism

1. Shayna Englin and Stefan Hankin, "The Advocacy Gap: Research for Better Advocacy," Englin Consulting, 2012.

2. Englin and Hankin, "The Advocacy Gap," 6.

3. John Larsen, "Emissions Reductions Under Cap-and-trade Proposals in the 111th Congress," World Resources Institute, June 8, 2010, 11.

Epilogue: Our Zero Footprint Baby

1. Mark Lino, "Expenditures on Children by Families in 2011," U.S. Department of Agriculture, Center for Nutrition Policy and Promotion, 2012.

Appendix 1

1. Cool Climate Network, "Cool Climate Carbon Footprint Calculator",http://coolclimate.berkeley.edu/carboncalculator.
2. U.S. Energy Information Administration, "Annual Energy Review", September 2012, http://www.eia.gov/totalenergy/data/annual/index.cfm.
3. Jonathan Koomey, "Growth in Data center electricity use 2005 to 2010," Analytics Press, 2011, http://www.analyticspress.com/datacenters.html

Appendix 2

1. Palmer, "It's smart to reuse baby items, aside from breast-milk pumps and car seats."
2. "Cost of Cloth Diapers," http://www.diaperdecisions.com/pages/cost_of_cloth_diapers.php.
3. U.S. Environmental Protection Agency, Climate Change Division, "Calculator," http://www.epa.gov/climatechange/ghgemissions/ind-calculator.html.
4. Ibid.
5. International Civil Aviation Organization, "ICAO Carbon Emissions Calculator."
6. U.S. Environmental Protection Agency, Climate Change Division, "Calculator."
7. Ibid.
8. The Union of Concerned Scientists , *Cooler Smarter: Practical Steps for Low-Carbon Living* (Washington, DC: Island Press, 2012).
9. Adoption.com, "The Costs of Adopting: A Factsheet for Families", http://costs.adoption.com/articles/the-costs-of-adopting-a-factsheet-for-families.html.